Mastery of Your Anxiety and Panic

✓ **Treatments** *That Work*™

Mastery of Your Anxiety and Panic

FOURTH EDITION

Workbook

David H. Barlow • Michelle G. Craske

UNIVERSITY PRESS

2007

OXFORD
UNIVERSITY PRESS

Oxford University Press, Inc., publishes works that further
Oxford University's objective of excellence
in research, scholarship, and education.

Oxford   New York
Auckland   Cape Town   Dar es Salaam   Hong Kong   Karachi
Kuala Lumpur   Madrid   Melbourne   Mexico City   Nairobi
New Delhi   Shanghai   Taipei   Toronto

With offices in
Argentina   Austria   Brazil   Chile   Czech Republic   France   Greece
Guatemala   Hungary   Italy   Japan   Poland   Portugal   Singapore
South Korea   Switzerland   Thailand   Turkey   Ukraine   Vietnam

Published by Oxford University Press, Inc.
198 Madison Avenue, New York, New York 10016

www.oup.com

Oxford is a registered trademark of Oxford University Press

ISBN-13 978-0-19-531135-8

ISBN 0-19-531135-3

9 8 7 6 5 4 3 2 1

Printed in the United States of America
on acid-free paper

About Treatments*ThatWork*™

One of the most difficult problems confronting patients with various disorders and diseases is finding the best help available. Everyone is aware of friends or family members who have sought treatment from a seemingly reputable practitioner, only to find out later from another doctor that the original diagnosis was wrong or that the treatments recommended were inappropriate or perhaps even harmful. Most patients or family members address this problem by reading everything they can about the patient's symptoms, seeking out information on the Internet, or aggressively "asking around" to tap knowledge from friends and acquaintances. Governments and healthcare policymakers are also aware that people in need do not always get the best treatments—something they refer to as "variability in healthcare practices."

Now healthcare systems around the world are attempting to correct this variability by introducing "evidence-based practice." This simply means that it is in everyone's interest that patients get the most up-to-date and effective care for a particular problem. Healthcare policymakers have also recognized that it is very useful to give consumers of healthcare as much information as possible, so that they can make intelligent decisions in a collaborative effort to improve health and mental health. This series, Treatments *ThatWork*™, is designed to accomplish just that. Only the latest and most effective interventions for particular problems are described in user-friendly language. To be included in this series, each treatment program must pass the highest standards of evidence available, as determined by a scientific advisory board. Thus, when individuals suffering from these problems or their family members seek out an expert clinician who is familiar with these interventions and decides that they are appropriate, they will have confidence that they are receiving the best care available. Of course, only your healthcare professional can decide on the right mix of treatments for you.

This particular program presents the latest version of a cognitive-behavioral treatment approach for panic disorder with or without agoraphobia.

There has been recognition in recent years that panic attacks are prevalent and that individuals suffering from panic disorder with varying levels of agoraphobia constitute 5–8 % of the population of the United States, with comparable figures now available from other countries around the world. As noted in this workbook, this means that one out of approximately every 12 people suffers from this devastating disorder at some time during his or her lifetime. In this workbook, you will join tens of thousands of individuals who have learned the skills to cope effectively with panic attacks and their devastating consequences and to master the emotional rollercoaster that is panic disorder. Ideally, we are all striving toward a goal of preventing the occurrence of panic disorder and associated anxiety. But for the time being, governments around the world and their health services have stipulated cognitive-behavioral treatments such as this one as the first-line approach in relieving the considerable suffering associated with panic disorder. In this, the fourth edition of this widely used workbook, further refinements are incorporated in order to take advantage of our ever-growing knowledge of the nature and successful treatment of panic disorder with agoraphobia. For example, focusing even more specifically on the extraordinarily frightening physical sensations that accompany panic attacks which are also associated with strong sensations of losing control are now an even more important part of the exercises in this workbook. As with all programs such as this, this workbook is most effectively applied under the direction of a clinician trained in this approach.

David H. Barlow, Editor-in-Chief,
Treatments *That Work*™
Boston, Massachusetts

Contents

Chapter 1

The Nature of Panic Disorder and Agoraphobia

Goals

- To understand the nature of panic attacks, panic disorder, and agoraphobia

- To learn about factors that cause panic disorder

- To learn about this program for overcoming panic and agoraphobia

- To determine whether or not this program is right for you

Do You Have Panic Disorder or Agoraphobia?

Do you have rushes of fear that make you think that you are sick, dying, or losing your mind? When these panicky feelings happen, does it feel as if your heart is going to burst out of your chest or as if you cannot get enough air? Or maybe you feel dizzy, faint, trembly, sweaty, short of breath, or just scared to death. Do the feelings sometimes come from out of the blue, when you least expect them? Are you worried about when these feelings will happen again? Do these feelings interfere with your normal daily routine or prevent you from doing things that you would normally do?

If these descriptions apply to you, then you may be suffering from panic disorder and agoraphobia. The rushes of fear are called *panic attacks.* Usually, panic attacks are accompanied by general anxiety about the possibility of another attack. Together, the panic attacks and general anxiety are called *panic disorder. Agoraphobia* refers to anxiety about, or avoidance of, situations where panic attacks or other physical symptoms are expected to occur. These terms are described in more detail later. Here are some examples of how panic disorder and agoraphobia can affect people's lives.

Steve

◼ *Steve was a 31-year-old sales manager who suffered from attacks of dizziness, blurred vision, and heart palpitations. The first panic attack occurred at work, in the presence of his coworkers, and began with feelings of weakness, nausea, and dizziness. Steve asked a colleague to call a doctor because he was afraid that he was having a heart attack since his father had recently died of one. In addition to this personal loss, Steve was dealing with a lot of stress at work. Several months before the first panic attack, there were times when Steve had been nervous and his writing had become shaky; but apart from that, he had never experienced anything like this before. After a thorough physical examination, his doctor told him that it was stress and anxiety. Nevertheless, the panics continued, mostly at work, and in trapped situations. Sometimes they were unexpected or "out of the blue," particularly the ones that woke him out of deep sleep. Steve felt tense and anxious most of the time because he worried about having another panic attack. Since his third panic attack, Steve had begun to avoid being alone whenever possible. He also avoided places and situations, such as stores, shopping malls, crowds, theaters, and waiting in lines, where he feared being trapped and embarrassed if he panicked. Wherever he went, Steve carried a Bible, as well as chewing gum and cigarettes, because glancing at the Bible, chewing gum, or smoking cigarettes made him feel more comfortable and better able to cope. In addition, Steve took medication with him wherever he went to help deal with his panic attacks.* ◼

Lisa

◼ *Lisa was a 24-year-old woman who had repeated attacks of dizziness, breathlessness, chest pain, blurred vision, a lump in her throat, and feelings of unreality. She was afraid that these feelings meant that something was wrong with her brain, such as a tumor, or that she was losing control of her mind. The problem began about five years before. While at a party, Lisa smoked some marijuana, and within a short while, she began to feel very unreal and dizzy. Never having had these feelings before, Lisa thought that she was going insane or that the drug had damaged her brain. She asked a friend* to take her to the emergency room. The physicians did some tests and reassured Lisa that her symptoms were due to anxiety. Lisa never touched marijuana or other recreational drugs after that. In fact, she became nervous about any chemical substances, even ones prescribed for allergies and sinus infections. The panic attacks waxed and waned over the years. At one point, she had no attacks for three months. However, she continued to worry about having another panic attack almost all of the time. She felt uneasy in situations where it would be difficult to get help if another panic attack occurred, such as in unfamiliar places or when she was alone, but she did not actually avoid many places. Her method of coping with panic was to get as involved as she could in other things so as to keep her mind off panic. ■

Judy

■ Judy was a 41-year-old, married woman who was unemployed because of her panic attacks. Judy quit her job as a paralegal several years ago because it had become increasingly difficult for her to leave her house. Judy's panic attacks involved strong chest pains and feelings of pressure on her chest, numbness in her left arm, shortness of breath, and heart palpitations. Each time she panicked, Judy was terrified that she was dying of a heart attack. In addition, Judy frequently woke up out of deep sleep with similar feelings, particularly pressure on her chest, shortness of breath, and sweating. Judy lived with her extended family, which was of Chinese descent and believed that the nighttime events represented demons descending on her. Her grandmother convinced Judy that she would die if she did not wake up in time. Consequently, Judy became very afraid to go to sleep. She would spend many hours pacing the floors when everyone else was asleep. Instead, she napped throughout the day, when other people were around. Her life had become very restricted to the house, with occasional outings to stores and doctors as long as a family member or friend accompanied her. Judy had seen many doctors and cardiologists, and she had undergone several cardiovascular stress tests and a halter recording to measure her heart over extended periods of time. Nothing was detected, and yet Judy remained convinced that she would have a heart attack or that she would die in her sleep. ■

The mental health classification system used in the United States and many other countries, referred to as the *Diagnostic and Statistical Manual for Mental Disorders,* fourth edition, text revision (*DSM-IV-TR;* APA, 2000), identifies the problem addressed in this workbook as panic disorder with or without agoraphobia. The key features of panic disorder are: (1) one or more episodes of abrupt, intense fear or discomfort (i.e., a panic attack); and (2) persistent anxiety or worry about the recurrence of panic attacks, their consequences, or life changes as a result of the attacks.

Panic attacks refer to an abrupt rush of intense fear or discomfort accompanied by a number of physical and cognitive symptoms, which are listed below. Occasional panic attacks are common. However, not everyone who experiences occasional panic attacks develops panic disorder. Details about the frequency of panic attacks and panic disorder in the general population are described in a later section.

Panic Attack Symptoms

- Shortness of breath or smothering sensations

- Heart palpitations or a racing or pounding heart

- Chest pain or discomfort

- Trembling or shaking

- Feelings of choking

- Sweating

- Feeling dizzy, unsteady, lightheaded, or faint

- Hot or cold flashes

- Nausea or abdominal distress

- Feelings of unreality or detachment

- Numbness or tingling

- Fears of dying

- Fears of going insane or losing control

Panic attacks occur as a part of many different anxiety problems. However, in other anxiety problems, panic attacks usually are *not* what the person is most worried about. In panic disorder, the panic attacks become the major source of concern and worry.

Continuing with the technical definition of panic disorder, at least one of the panic attacks must be unexpected or occur for no real reason. In other words, the panic seems to occur from "out of the blue." A good example of an unexpected panic attack is an attack that occurs when relaxing or when deeply asleep. For some people, panic attacks continue to occur unexpectedly, and for other people, the panic attacks eventually become tied to specific situations.

Another feature of panic disorder is avoiding, hesitating about, or feeling very nervous in situations where panic attacks or other physical symptoms (such as diarrhea) are expected to occur. Typically, these situations are ones where you may not be able to escape or find help. A common example is a crowded shopping mall, where it might be hard to find the exit and difficult to get through all the people if one has to leave suddenly because of a panic attack. A list of typical agoraphobia situations is provided in the list below. Avoiding situations because of fear when no real danger exists is called a *phobia*. Avoiding situations from which escape might be difficult or where help may be unavailable in the event of a panic attack or other physical symptoms is called *agoraphobia*. This is fitting because the *agora* was the ancient Greek marketplace—the original shopping mall. However, as can be seen from the list below, places and situations avoided by people with agoraphobia are not limited to malls.

Typical Agoraphobia Situations

- Driving

- Traveling by subway, bus, or taxi

- Flying

- Waiting in lines

- Crowds

- Stores

- Restaurants

- Theaters

- Long distances from home

- Unfamiliar areas

- Hairdressing salon or barbershop

- Long walks

- Wide, open spaces

- Closed-in spaces (e.g., basements)

- Boats

- Being at home alone

- Auditoriums

- Elevators

- Escalators

In most cases, agoraphobia develops after panic attacks, resulting in *panic disorder with agoraphobia.* However, some people never develop agoraphobia; they have *panic disorder without agoraphobia.* Occasionally, agoraphobia is present without panic attacks, in which case the official term is *agoraphobia without history of panic disorder.* In this case, the person may experience one, two, or three symptoms from the list of panic attack symptoms but never has had four or more symptoms at one time (which is the technical requirement for a full-blown panic attack). Nevertheless, one or two symptoms can be as distressing as four or more symptoms. For example, lightheadedness is sometimes the only symptom experienced, but anxiety about feeling lightheaded can be as severe and disabling as the anxiety about having a full-blown panic attack. Putting it another way, the person who has lightheadedness only may end up becoming as agoraphobic as the person who has lightheadedness plus many other panic attack symptoms.

Another example of agoraphobia without panic disorder is when abdominal distress is the primary symptom, resulting in hesitation about entering situations where restrooms are not easily accessible. Abdominal distress may be part of *irritable bowel syndrome,* which involves a chronic disturbance in bowel habits and includes nausea, stomach cramping, constipation, or diarrhea. These types of symptoms are not due to a medical condition and are often intensified by stress, such as the stress of an agoraphobia situation.

Agoraphobia without history of panic disorder also refers to avoidance of situations because of other bodily symptoms that are not on the list of panic attack symptoms, such as visual disturbances. A list of these symptoms is shown here.

Other Physical Symptoms That Might Lead to Agoraphobia

- Headaches

- Tunnel vision or sensitivity to light

- Muscle spasms

- Urinary retention problems

- Weakness

- Fatigue

- Diarrhea

- Sensations of falling

The overriding notion is that agoraphobia comes from being anxious about uncomfortable physical symptoms in certain situations. These situations are ones in which it seems difficult to cope with the uncomfortable feelings because of the feelings of being trapped or of there being no way of getting help.

It is possible to be anxious about and avoid these types of situations for reasons unrelated to uncomfortable physical symptoms. For example, many people refuse to fly because of concerns about crashing or being hijacked. Or, difficulty driving can be based on concerns about being hit by other drivers. Similarly, avoidance of being alone or of leaving one's safety zone can be related to concerns of being attacked, mugged, or other external dangers. This workbook is *not* written with these kinds of fears in mind. Instead, this workbook is for fear and avoidance behavior due to uncomfortable physical symptoms and panic attacks.

Certain medical problems can cause panic attacks, and controlling them eliminates panic attacks. These medical problems include hyperthyroidism (overactive thyroid gland) and pheochromocytoma (a tumor on the adrenal gland, which is very rare). Other medical problems include extreme use of amphetamines (such as benzedrine, which is sometimes prescribed for asthma or weight loss) or caffeine (10 or more cups of coffee per day). However, these medical problems are different from panic disorder. In panic disorder, the panic attacks are not caused by medical problems. (We recommend that those who feel that they are suffering from panic attacks undergo a full physical exam to decide whether the panic attacks are caused by these types of medical problems or whether they are part of panic disorder.)

There are other medical problems that cause panic-like symptoms, but controlling these medical problems does not eliminate panic attacks. These include hypoglycemia (low blood sugar), mitral valve prolapse (flutter of the heart), asthma, allergies, and gastrointestinal problems (such as irritable bowel syndrome). It is possible to have one of these medical problems as well as panic disorder. For example, low blood-sugar levels may cause weakness and shakiness and thus lead to panic, but correction of blood-sugar levels through diet does not necessarily stop all panic attacks. In other words, these types of medical problems may be a complicating factor that exists alongside panic disorder, but removing these medical problems does not always remove panic disorder.

If you have not had medical tests in the past year, it may be wise to undergo a full medical examination to check for possible physical causes of panic-like symptoms and to identify other physical conditions that might contribute to panic and anxiety. These factors can then be taken into account during the treatment program.

How Common Are Panic Disorder and Agoraphobia?

Panic attacks and agoraphobia are very common. The most recent large-scale surveys of the adult population of the United States show that from 5 to 8% of individuals experience panic disorder and/or agoraphobia at some time in their lives. This means that somewhere between 15 and 25 million people in the United States alone suffer from panic disorder and/or agoraphobia.

One out of every 12 people suffers from panic disorder and/or agoraphobia at some time in his or her life.

In addition, many people have occasional panic attacks that do not develop into panic disorder. For example, over 30% of the population has had a panic attack during the past year, usually in response to a stressful situation, such as an examination or a car accident. Moreover, a significant number of people experience occasional panic attacks from "out of the blue" or for no real reason—estimates range from 3 to 14% in the last year.

Panic attacks and agoraphobia occur in all kinds of people, across all social and educational levels, professions, and types of persons. They are also present across different races and cultures, although panics may be described and understood differently according to specific cultural beliefs. Recognition of panic disorder in other cultures has led to the translation of this workbook into several other languages, including Chinese, Spanish, Korean, and Arabic.

Unhelpful Ways of Coping With Panic Attacks

We already mentioned a common way of coping with panic attacks: avoiding situations where they might occur (i.e., agoraphobia). Although avoidance of situations decreases anxiety in the short term, in the long term it contributes to anxiety. The same is true for several others ways of coping with panic attacks, including distractions, superstitious objects and safety signals, and alcohol.

Avoidance

In addition to avoidance of situations from which escape is difficult or help is not easily available (i.e., agoraphobia), avoidance extends to avoiding activities and other things. For example, consider the following behaviors.

- Do you avoid drinking coffee?

- Do you avoid medication of any kind, even if prescribed by your doctor?

- Do you avoid exercise or physical exertion?

- Do you avoid becoming very angry?

- Do you avoid sexual relations?

- Do you avoid watching horror movies, medical documentaries, or very sad movies?

- Do you avoid being outside in very hot or very cold conditions?

- Do you avoid being away from medical help?

- Do you avoid being rushed?

Usually, these activities are avoided because they produce symptoms that are similar to panic attack symptoms. Again, while avoidance helps relieve anxiety and panic in the short term, it contributes to anxiety in the long term.

Distraction

Many people attempt to "get through" anxious situations by distracting themselves. There is no limit to the methods used for distraction. For example, if you feel yourself becoming anxious or panicky, do you:

- Play loud music?

- Carry around something to read?

- Pinch yourself?

- Snap an elastic band on your wrist?

- Place cold, wet towels on your face?

- Tell somebody who is with you to talk about something—anything?

- Keep as busy as possible?

- Keep the television on as you go to sleep?

- Imagine yourself somewhere else?

- Play counting games?

Chances are that these types of distractions have helped you get through a panic attack in the past and may well help you in the future. However, they can become a crutch. For example, if you forget your reading material or your elastic band, you may have to go home to get it. Also, in the long run, these strategies are not very helpful. Distraction is like placing tape around a broken table leg without fixing the break. We will discuss this further in chapter 5.

Superstitious Objects and Safety Signals

Superstitious objects or people are specific items or persons that make one feel safe. (They are also called *safety signals.*) Examples include other people, food, or empty or full medication bottles. If these objects or people were *not* around, you would probably feel more anxious. The reality is these superstitious objects do not actually "save" you because there is really nothing to be saved from. Other superstitious objects are listed below.

Superstitious Objects and Safety Signals

- Food or drink
- Smelling salts
- Paper bags
- Religious symbols
- Flashlights
- Money
- Cameras
- Bags or purses
- Reading material
- Cigarettes
- Pets
- Portable phones

As with distractions, these objects become a crutch and can contribute to anxiety in the long run.

Alcohol

Perhaps you use a far more dangerous coping strategy—alcohol. We now know that many men (moreso than women) drink to get through situations where they might have a panic attack. In fact, from one third to one half of people with alcohol problems began the long road to alcohol addiction by "self-medicating" anxiety or panic. Using alcohol to cope with your panics and anxiety is extremely dangerous. This is because while alcohol works for a little while, you are likely to become dependent on the alcohol and require more and more of it. As you drink more and more, the anxiety-reducing properties of alcohol become less and less. Instead, anxiety and depression tend to increase. If you drink to control your anxiety, make every effort to stop as soon as possible, and ask your doctor or mental health professional for help.

How Does This Program Help You Cope With Panic and Agoraphobia?

Instead of relying on avoidance, distractions, superstitious objects, alcohol, or other unhelpful methods, this program is designed to educate you and to teach constructive ways of coping. This program focuses on ways of coping with panic, anxiety about panic, and avoidance of panic. The kind of treatment that is described in this program is called *cognitive-behavioral therapy* (CBT). CBT differs from traditional psychotherapies in several important ways.

Unlike traditional psychotherapies, CBT teaches skills to manage anxiety and panic. Specifically, you will be taught ways of slowing your breathing, ways of changing the way you think, and ways of facing the things that make you anxious so that they no longer bother you. For each set of skills, we begin with educational information and then outline exercises to be practiced. Then, we build on the previous practice by developing new skills. Finally, the skills are used to cope with panic and anxiety.

Unlike traditional psychotherapies, you will be given homework assignments. Thus, CBT is much like attending class and continuing to learn on your own by further study between classes. In many ways, it is the self-study program that is the most essential to your success.

Unlike traditional psychotherapies, we do not emphasize your childhood memories and experiences (unless they are directly related to your panic attacks, as might occur if witnessing someone die of a heart attack when you were a child led you to fear that you will also die of a heart attack). Instead, CBT emphasizes interruption of the factors that currently contribute to your panic disorder and agoraphobia. As you will see, it is this method that has proven to be highly effective.

A good beginning to CBT is education about what causes panic attacks.

What Causes Panic, Anxiety, and Agoraphobia?

The question of what causes panic, anxiety, and agoraphobia is very difficult, and we do not know all of the answers just yet. We will discuss the subject in more detail in chapter 2, but it is important to say several things here about the causes of panic and anxiety.

Biological Factors

First, the research does not suggest that panic attacks are due to a biological disease. Of course, there are the relatively rare examples mentioned above where a medical condition does cause symptoms that resemble a panic attack, such as hyperthyroidism or a tumor on the adrenal gland. However, common panic attacks do not seem to be due to biological dysfunction.

Many people ask whether panic attacks are due to a chemical imbalance. Neurochemicals are substances in the central nervous system, including the brain, which are involved in sending nerve impulses. Neurochemicals that may influence panic and anxiety include noradrenalin and serotonin. While these types of substances may be present in greater amounts in the midst of anxiety and panic, there is no evidence to suggest that a neurochemical imbalance is the original or main cause of panic and anxiety. Some recent evidence using "brain scan" procedures called Positron Emission Topography (PET) and functional magnetic resonance imaging (fMRI) has shown that certain parts of the brain seem to be particularly active in anxious patients. However, it is not at all clear whether these findings are the effect of anxiety or the cause of anxiety.

On the other hand, certain biological factors that may be inherited or passed on through genes may lead some people to be more likely to panic. Many believe that what is inherited are overly sensitive parts of the nervous system which lead to a tendency to experience all negative emotions, including anger, sadness, guilt, and shame, as well as anxiety and panic. However, inheriting vulnerabilities to experience negative emotions does not guarantee that you will experience panic attacks or panic disorder. In other words, panic is not inherited in the same way that, say, eye color is inherited. If you inherit the genetic structure for blue eyes, then you will have blue eyes. You do not, however, inherit panic disorder in this way. People probably inherit a tendency (or a vulnerability) to panic disorder—something that increases the chances of developing panic disorder but does not guarantee it. Furthermore, even with a vulnerability to panic, it is possible to think and act in ways that prevent panic attacks from recurring (which is exactly what we teach in this program).

Biological factors (whatever they may be) probably help explain why panic disorder tends to run in families. In other words, if one family member has panic disorder, then another person in the same family is more likely to have panic disorder than are others in the general population. That is, whereas 5–8% of the U.S. population has panic disorder and/or agoraphobia, 15–20% of first-degree relatives (parents, siblings, children) of someone with panic disorder themselves develop panic disorder.

Psychological Factors

Psychological factors are important also. People who experience panic attacks tend to have certain beliefs that lead them to be especially afraid of physical symptoms, such as racing heart, shortness of breath, dizziness, and so on. The beliefs are that physical symptoms are harmful, either mentally, physically, or socially. Examples of such beliefs include thoughts that a racing heart could mean heart disease, that lightheadedness could mean that you are about to pass out, that a growling stomach could mean you will lose control of your bowels, that strong emotions mean that you are out of control, or that a sense of unreality means that you are losing control of your mind or going insane.

The sources of these beliefs are not fully known, but personal experiences with health and illness may be one important contributor. For example, parents who are overprotective about their child's physical health may contribute to a general overconcern about physical well-being in the child that gradually develops into beliefs that physical symptoms are harmful. Or, the sudden and unexpected loss of close family members to physical problems, such as heart attacks or stroke, may increase the likelihood that someone believes that their own physical symptoms are harmful. Another example is to observe another family member suffer through a prolonged, serious illness.

However, beliefs are not the sole cause of panic attacks. As with the biological factors described previously, beliefs that physical symptoms are harmful probably increase the likelihood of panic attacks and panic disorder but do not guarantee them. Furthermore, this type of psychological vulnerability can be offset by learning to think and act in different ways.

Most likely, the vulnerability to panic is based on a complex interaction between psychological and biological factors. What we do know is that a panic attack is a surge of fear that by itself is a normal bodily response. What makes it abnormal is that it occurs at the wrong time; that is, when there is no real reason to be afraid. Again, the response itself is normal and natural, and it would be the same kind of reaction you would have if you were to face a real danger (such as being attacked by a person with a gun). In addition, it is normal and natural to become anxious about having another panic attack and to avoid places where you think that panic attacks are likely to occur, if you believe that panic attacks are harmful to you.

What About Stress?

For most people, their first panic attack happened when they were under a lot of stress. In addition to negative stressful events, such as job loss, stress can be positive as well, such as moving to a new home, having a baby, or getting married. This probably explains why panic attacks are more likely to begin in the 20s, since that is when we tend to take on new responsibilities, such as leaving home and starting new careers and relationships.

During stressful periods, everyone is more tense, and even little things become harder to manage. Stress can increase overall levels of physical tension and can lower your confidence in your ability to cope with life. Additionally, having to deal with many negative life stresses can cause us to think of the world as a threatening or dangerous place. For all these reasons, a situation that may normally be very manageable becomes much more stressful when it occurs in the context of other ongoing stress. Think of a woman who has recently lost her job and whose marriage is breaking up. Within that background of stress, it may be much more difficult for her to deal with traffic delays than if there were no background stress. So, as a result, stress increases the chances of panic attacks. However, stress alone is not an adequate explanation. Some people do not panic even though they are under a lot of stress. Instead, they have other reactions to stress, such as headaches, high blood pressure, or ulcers. It seems that stressful events increase the likelihood of panic attacks in people who are vulnerable or susceptible to panic. These vulnerabilities include the biological and psychological factors already described.

Furthermore, stress is rarely the reason why panic attacks persist. For example, although panic attacks may have begun during a time of a lot of marital problems, they are likely to continue even after the marital problems have been resolved. This is because panic attacks and anxiety tend to take on a negative, self-maintaining cycle of their own. This set of maintenance cycles is described in detail in chapter 2.

Is This Program Right for You?

The following list will help you to determine whether you can benefit from this program.

Consider if you have experienced any of the following.

■ Episodes of abrupt and extreme discomfort or fear (i.e., panic)

■ At least some of the panic attacks include physical symptoms and fears, such as:

   ■ Shortness of breath or smothering
   ■ Heart palpitations or racing or pounding heart
   ■ Chest pain or discomfort
   ■ Trembling or shaking
   ■ Feelings of choking
   ■ Sweating
   ■ Feeling dizzy, unsteady, lightheaded or faint
   ■ Chills or hot flushes
   ■ Nausea or abdominal distress
   ■ Feelings of unreality or detachment
   ■ Numbness or tingling

- Fears of dying
- Fears of going insane or losing control

- At least one panic attack was unexpected or came from out of the blue

- Persistent anxiety or worry about panic attacks, their consequences, or life changes as a result of the attacks

- Avoidance of different situations (such as driving, being alone, crowded areas, unfamiliar areas) or activities (such as exercise) in which you expect to panic

- The panic attacks are not the direct result of physical conditions or diseases

As already mentioned, panic attacks can be a part of all types of anxiety problems, such as social phobia, obsessive-compulsive disorder (OCD), generalized anxiety, posttraumatic stress disorder (PTSD), and specific phobias. Panic attacks may also occur in mood disorders, such as depression. The distinguishing feature of panic disorder is that the panic attacks themselves become the main source of anxiety and concern. If you experience panic attacks but are not anxious about having panic attacks, and instead, you are worried about other things, then consult with your mental health professional to learn if a different treatment is more appropriate. You fit this program if your main concern is the panic attacks themselves and, of course, if the panic attacks are not the direct result of physical conditions or diseases.

Are You Receiving Other Psychological Treatments?

This program may be appropriate for you even if you have had contact with other mental health professionals in the past for panic and anxiety. We have used this program time and time again with people who have been through many different forms of treatment. However, some consideration must be given to other treatment that is ongoing with your participation in this program. We recommend that this program not be combined with other psychotherapy that specifically addresses your panic and anxiety. The reason for this is that messages from different treatments for the same problem can become mixed and confusing. We find it much more effective to do only one therapy for panic disorder at a time. On the other hand, if you are receiving ongoing general therapy or therapy focused on a different problem area (such as marital problems), then there is no reason why you cannot participate in this program as well.

If you are involved in another psychotherapy that specifically addresses your panic attacks and anxiety, we recommend that you pursue that treatment until you are sure that either it is effective (in which case, no more treatment is needed) or that it is ineffective (in which case, our program can be tried). As you will soon see, our program has been shown to be very effective for many people, but that does not mean that other psychotherapies should not be given a fair trial. Different forms of therapy are more or less effective for different people. You must make this decision if you are involved in another treatment for panic disorder and agoraphobia. To aid this decision, the National Institute for Mental Health published an official statement in 1991 in which it was recommended that decisions about whether psychological treatments for panic disorder are beneficial or not should be made after about six weeks, when the beginnings of improvements should be evident. Furthermore, they recommended against continuing for years in psychotherapy for panic disorder when there is no evidence for improvement.

Are You Taking Medications?

This program will be appropriate even if you use medications to control your anxiety and panic, assuming that despite the medication, you continue to be anxious about panic attacks. We say this because medications are not always fully effective. For some people, medications are only mildly to moderately effective or not effective at all. For others, medications are effective initially, but then relapse occurs when the medication is stopped.

Fortunately, medication treatments can be successfully combined with this program, and we discuss ways of achieving this in chapter 10. In addition, this program has been found to be helpful for persons who want to stop their medications. For those who have an interest in stopping their medications, we make some suggestions in chapter 10 that can be combined with direct medical supervision of the withdrawal process. It is definitely not wise to stop taking medication on your own.

In this program, you will learn how to manage your panic attacks, anxiety about panic, and avoidance of panic and agoraphobia situations. The program is divided into 11 chapters, and several of the chapters have a number of different sections. In each chapter, you will learn specific skills. An outline of the content of each chapter is presented below. The skills build upon each other, so that in each new chapter or each new section, you will use skills that you have learned previously. The program is obviously structured, but there is room for individual tailoring.

A self-assessment section at the end of each chapter or each section lets you test whether you have understood the information. If you have not, go back over the material again. This is important, because each new step is based on the previous steps. If you have understood the material presented in the chapter or chapter section, then continue to the next. In addition, homework exercises are outlined at the end of each chapter or section. Their importance cannot be emphasized enough, as the success of the program is based largely on your completing them.

The pacing is somewhat up to you, but we recommend the following general pace. The first phase, called the *Basics,* takes one week, in which you are to read chapters 2–4 and the first section of chapter 11. These chapters provide all the necessary background information for you to begin learning specific strategies and will also get you going in terms of recording your panic and anxiety. After at least a full week of recording, you begin the *Coping Skills* phase that is devoted to developing your hierarchy of agoraphobia situations (chapter 5) and learning regulatory breathing (chapter 6) and thinking skills (chapter 7). The Coping Skills phase should take about three weeks. Then, the subsequent six weeks or so should be devoted to the *Exposure* phase, which involves repeated practice in facing agoraphobia situations (chapters 8 and 9) and facing frightening physical symptoms (chapter 10). The amount of time in the *Exposure* phase is very much dependent on the number of agoraphobia situations and the number of symptoms which cause you to feel anxious. Considerations about how to stop medication (chapter 11, section 2) and strategies to maintain your progress in the long term (chapter 12) are covered in the last phase, *Planning for the Future.* Here is the list of chapters:

Chapter 1.   Introduction

Basics

Chapter 2.   Learning to Record Panic and Anxiety

Chapter 3.   Negative Cycles of Panic and Agoraphobia

Chapter 4.   Panic Attacks Are Not Harmful

Coping Skills

Chapter 5.   Establishing Your Hierarchy of Agoraphobia Situations

Chapter 6.   Breathing Skills

Chapter 7.   Thinking Skills

Exposure

Chapter 8.   Facing Agoraphobia Situations

Chapter 9.   Involving Others

Chapter 10.   Facing Physical Symptoms

Planning for the Future

Chapter 11.   Medications

Chapter 12.   Accomplishments, Maintenance, and Relapse Prevention

The following outline presents a recommended pace, although you should once again recognize that the pace is likely to shift based on your own profile of panic, anxiety, and agoraphobia. For example, you will spend much less time on chapter 8 if you avoid only a limited number of agoraphobia situations.

Week 1   Chapter 2: Learning to Record Panic and Anxiety

Chapter 3: Negative Cycles of Panic and Agoraphobia

Chapter 4: Panic Attacks Are Not Harmful

Chapter 11, Section 1: Medications (Education)

Week 2   Chapter 5: Establishing Your Hierarchy of Agoraphobia Situations

Chapter 6, Section 1: Breathing Skills (Diaphragmatic Breathing)

Chapter 7, Sections 1 and 2: Thinking Skills (Basics; Realistic Odds)

Week 3	Chapter 6, Section 2: Breathing Skills (Slow Breathing)
	Chapter 7, Section 3: Thinking Skills (Putting Things Into Perspective)
Week 4	Chapter 6, Section 3: Breathing Skills (Coping Application)
	Chapter 7, Section 4: Thinking Skills (Review; Memories)
	Chapter 8, Section 1: Facing Agoraphobia Situations (Planning)
	Chapter 9: Involving Significant Others
Week 5	Chapter 6, Section 4: Breathing Skills (Review)
	Chapter 8, Section 2: Facing Agoraphobia Situations (Review and Planning)
	Chapter 10, Section 1: Facing Physical Symptoms (Assessment and Practice)
Week 6	Chapter 8, Section 2: Facing Agoraphobia Situations (Review and Planning)
	Chapter 10, Section 2: Facing Physical Symptoms (Review and Practice)
Week 7	Chapter 8, Section 2: Facing Agoraphobia Situations (Review and Planning)
	Chapter 10, Section 2: Facing Physical Symptoms (Review and Practice)
Week 8	Chapter 8, Section 2: Facing Agoraphobia Situations (Review and Planning)
	Chapter 10, Section 3: Facing Physical Symptoms (Review and Practice, Activities Planning)
Week 9	Chapter 8, Section 2: Facing Agoraphobia Situations (Review and Planning)
	Chapter 10, Section 3: Facing Physical Symptoms (Review and Practice, Activities Planning)

Week 10   Chapter 8, Section 3: Facing Agoraphobia Situations (Symptoms)

Chapter 10, Section 3: Facing Physical Symptoms (Review and Practice, Activities Planning)

Week 11   Chapter 8, Section 3: Facing Agoraphobia Situations (Symptoms)

Chapter 10, Section 3: Facing Physical Symptoms (Review and Practice, Activities Planning)

Week 12   Chapter 11, Section 2: Medications (Stopping Medications)

Chapter 12: Accomplishments, Maintenance, and Relapse Prevention

Finally, we recommend that you work on this program with your doctor or mental health professional. That person can provide additional information, advice, and guidance as you learn the various skills and conduct the different exercises. Furthermore, your doctor or mental health professional can help to tailor the program to your own needs.

For the period of time that you give to this program, it must become a priority. Just as up until this time, fear has been your major focus, achieving mastery of your anxiety and panic should now be your major focus.

What Benefits Will You Receive From This Program?

What should you expect to get out of this program? This information is important in your decision to participate in our program. Research that we have conducted over the last 20 years shows this treatment to be very successful. The percentage of people who report that they are free of panic at the completion of a program similar to this one is 70–90%. This rate of success has been replicated by other researchers around the world who have tested treatments similar to this one. What is even more exciting is that these results seem to persist over long periods of time—up to 24 months after treatment, which is the longest period we have examined. One of the reasons for this long-term benefit is that the treatment is essentially a learning program. When something is learned, it becomes a natural part of your reactions and therefore is carried with you even after the formal program has been completed. You may have ups and downs, but by completing this program, you will be able to handle the downs much more effectively and return to normal functioning more easily.

On the basis of results obtained as early as 1991, the National Institute of Mental Health came out with an official statement recognizing that the treatments of choice for panic disorder are either this type of program (CBT) and/or medication therapy. Obviously, there is never a guarantee that this treatment will be the one for you or that you may never panic again, but from the success rates, it would seem that this program is worth trying.

These numbers refer to the success with which panic attacks are controlled. Remember that many people who panic develop agoraphobia as well. Treatment programs focused on agoraphobia per se produce significant improvements in 60–80% of our patients. Again, this rate of improvement is maintained—and, in fact, improvement usually continues—up to two years after treatment completion. (Again, this is the longest duration that we have evaluated.)

What Is the Cost?

Knowing how effective these programs are, the question for you becomes, "What is the cost?" Mainly, the cost is time and effort over the next 10–12 weeks. One (and perhaps the only) factor known to predict the effectiveness of this program is the amount of practice that is conducted. The more you put in, the more you will get out of the program. It is not the severity of your panic and avoidance, how long you have been panicking, or how old you are that predicts success; rather, it is your motivation to learn to change. Do you have the motivation at this time to give it your best shot? One point to keep in mind is that you are probably putting out as much energy and effort into trying to manage your life with panic and anxiety as you would by going through this program. But the big plus from this program is that the energy and effort result in positive changes.

If you really do not have the motivation right now, then it is better to wait, because you will be defeating yourself by beginning a program like this halfheartedly.

Finally, even if your fear and anxiety diminish quickly as you proceed through the program, we recommend that you finish the program. It will

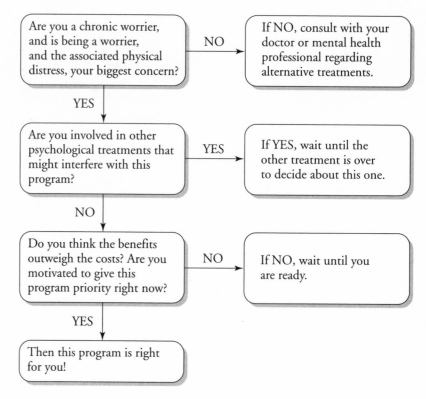

Figure 1.1.
Decision Tree

prove more effective in the long run to complete the entire program, in the same way that it is more effective to complete a prescription of an antibiotic even if bacterial symptoms clear up early on.

Homework

✎ Read chapters 2–4 and chapter 11, section 1.

Self-Assessment

Answer each of the following by circling T (True) or F (False). Answers are given in the appendix.

1. It is possible for people to have panic attacks but not have a diagnosis of panic disorder.   T   F

2. In addition to the unpleasant physical symptoms, panic attacks involve thoughts of going insane, losing control, or dying.   T   F

3. Panic attacks and agoraphobia are very rare problems, affecting less than 1% of the population.   T   F

4. Children of parents who have panic disorder are at no greater risk for developing panic disorder than children whose parents do not have panic disorder.   T   F

5. Superstitious objects, distractions, alcohol, and methods of avoidance have one thing in common—they contribute to anxiety and panic in the long term.   T   F

6. You are born with panic disorder, and there is nothing you can do about it once you have the genes for it.   T   F

Chapter 2

Learning to Record Panic and Anxiety

Goals

- To learn the importance of record-keeping

- To learn ways to record panic, anxiety, and other moods

Record-Keeping

This chapter presents the importance and method of record-keeping. For the rest of the time that you are involved with this program, you are asked to keep ongoing records of your panic and anxiety, among other things. Record-keeping is necessary to the success of this program.

Why Take the Time to Record? I Know I Am Anxious!

There are many reasons why it is important to keep records of your anxiety on a regular, ongoing basis. First, panic attacks, particularly those that seem to occur for no real reason, make people feel as if they are out of control and victims of their own anxiety. Learning to be an observer as opposed to a victim of your own anxiety is a first step toward gaining control. Through record-keeping, you will learn to observe when, where, and under what circumstances your panic and anxiety occur.

You will learn whether your panic attacks occur when you are alone or with others, after a stressful day at work or on weekends, in the middle of the day or at the end of the day; whether your panic attacks are brought on by feelings of excitement from watching a sports event on television, feeling overheated by a crowded shopping area, feeling suffocation from a steamy shower, thinking about horrible things that could happen, or by relaxing and having nothing else to do but dwell on your fears. Again, gaining an understanding of the factors that cause your panic and anxiety to escalate will lead you to feel more in control and like less of a victim.

Second, you will learn to understand the way in which you experience panic and anxiety, in terms of what you think, what you feel, and what you do. This is very important, because this program is designed specifically to change anxious thinking, anxious feelings, and anxious behaviors. They cannot be changed without knowing exactly what they are.

Third, ongoing record-keeping provides much more accurate information than you get by just asking yourself, "How have I been feeling lately?" If you were asked to describe the last week, you may judge it to have been "very bad" when, in fact, there may have been several times when you felt relatively calm. When anxiety is on your mind so much, it is easy to forget about the times when you were not anxious. As you can probably see, thinking about the previous week as "very bad" and overlooking relatively "okay" times during the week are likely to make you feel worse and more anxious. In fact, such negative judgments about how you have been doing in general may contribute to ongoing anxiety. By keeping ongoing records, you will not only feel more in control but also feel less anxious by being forced to recognize that your mood state fluctuates and that there are times when you feel less anxious than other times.

Finally, recording helps you to evaluate progress. For this reason, we recommend that you continuously record throughout the entire program. Continuous recording will let you appreciate the gains you make and will help to prevent occasional panic attacks from overshadowing the progress you have made.

Let us review all of the benefits of ongoing recording, as well as the reasons why it is crucial to this program:

■ to help you feel more in control, by being able to identify when and where panic attacks are more likely to happen;

■ identify the specific ways in which you experience anxiety; your physical feelings, your thoughts, and your behaviors;

■ to be able to judge your level of anxiety and panic more accurately;

■ to evaluate the success of your attempts to change.

What Is Objective Recording?

Sometimes, people are concerned that by continually recording their panic and anxiety, they will be reminded of how anxious they feel, which in turn will make them feel even more anxious. To address this concern, it is important to distinguish between two ways of recording: subjective recording and objective recording.

Subjective recording means recording "how bad you feel," how terrible the panic attacks are, how much they interfere with your life, or how you cannot control them. Examples include statements such as "I don't feel well, I could panic today; what if I get so dizzy that I have to go home?" Or, "I am really anxious. I wish these feelings would go away. What if they get worse?" This type of subjective recording tends to increase anxiety. Subjective recording is likely to be something that you already do and, at the same time, may be something that you try to avoid because it worsens your overall anxiety.

Objective recording, which is the technique that you will be learning in this chapter, means recording the features of panic and anxiety in a concrete and nonjudgmental way. You will learn to record things such as the number or intensity of symptoms, the triggers of your panic, your thoughts, and your behavioral responses to panic.

At first, it may be difficult to switch from subjective to objective recording, and as you start to use the records, you may indeed notice an increase in your anxiety because you are focusing on your feelings in the old, subjective way. However, with practice, most people are able to shift to the objective mode. To help you do this, we have developed very specific forms on which very specific objective information is to be recorded. These will be described soon.

What Do I Record?

Panic Attacks

You will record your panic attacks using the Panic Attack Record shown here. You may photocopy the form from this book or download multiple copies from the Treatments *ThatWork*™ website (http://www.oup.com/

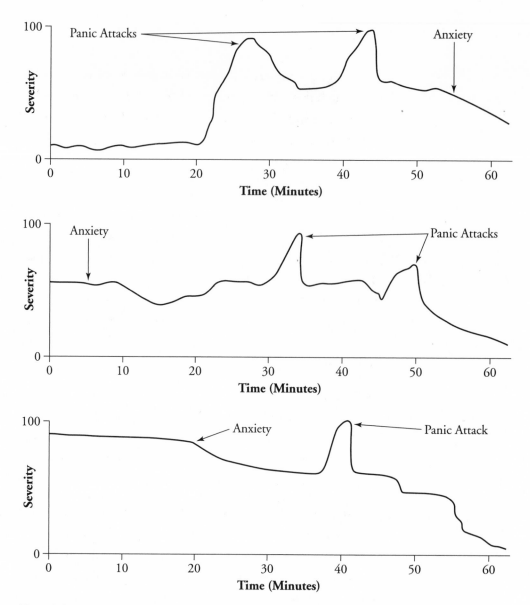

Figure 2.1.

Progression of Panic and Anxiety Over Time

us/ttw). Use this form whenever you experience a panic attack or a sudden rush of fear. Remember, panic is different from anxiety. Panic attacks are sudden rushes of fear, and they can happen when you are fully relaxed or when you are already anxious. Panic attacks peak quickly and then decrease within 10–30 minutes, although you may continue to feel some of the symptoms and to feel generally anxious for quite a while afterward. This is called *residual anxiety*. You may even panic again in the midst of the residual anxiety. (See Figure 2.1.)

In contrast, anxiety builds more slowly. At times, anxiety may be very intense and severe, as it would be before a surgery or while waiting for the results of a test. Anxiety is best described as worrying about something in the future, even if the future is only an hour away. Panic, on the other hand, is a rush of fear with thoughts of immediate catastrophe (e.g., "I am dying").

Do not wait until the end of the day to complete the Panic Attack Record, as you will lose the value of recording. Complete it as soon as possible after you panic. Of course, some circumstances, such as driving or talking in a meeting, make it hard to fill out the Panic Attack Record, but complete it as soon as possible.

On the Panic Attack Record, write down the date and the time that the panic attack began, and also note the triggers that seemed to bring on the panic attack. Triggers could include a stressful situation, an anxious thought, or an uncomfortable physical symptom. Even if you do not know what brought on your panic attack, list the thing that you noticed just before you panicked. You will also record whether the panic was unexpected or "out of the blue," as well as the maximum level of fear you experienced during the panic attack. Use a 10-point scale, where 0 = no fear, 5 = moderate fear, and 10 = extreme fear. You should also record each symptom that was present to at least a mild degree, your thoughts about what might happen, and your behaviors or what you did in response to the panic.

Examples of Panic Attack Records completed by Jill are shown here. Jill is 29 years old, married, and has one child. She began to panic one year ago, when her child was a few months old. Since then, she has been afraid to stay home alone with her baby and often spends the day at her mother's place, while her husband is at work. From Jill's first record, it can be seen that this panic occurred at 5:20 p.m. on February 16. She panicked while she was alone at home, waiting for her husband to return from work. She noted that the panic was brought on because she was home alone and felt short of breath. It was an expected panic; Jill was not surprised that she panicked because being home alone is a stressful situation for her. Her maximum fear rating was an 8, which is strong. Symptoms included racing heart, difficulty breathing, sweating, trembling and shaking, feelings of unreality, and a fear of losing control or going insane. Her thoughts were that she would lose control or go insane, and her behavioral response was to call her mother.

Panic Attack Record

Date: _____   Time began: _____

Triggers: _____

Expected: _____   Unexpected: _____

Maximum Fear

0 ------- 1 ------- 2 ------- 3 ------- 4 ------- 5 ------- 6 ------- 7 ------- 8 ------- 9 ------- 10

None   Mild   Moderate   Strong   Extreme

Check all symptoms present to at least a mild degree:

Chest pain or discomfort   _____

Sweating   _____

Heart racing/palpitations/pounding   _____

Nausea/upset stomach   _____

Shortness of breath   _____

Dizzy/unsteady/lightheaded/faint   _____

Shaking/trembling   _____

Chills/hot flushes   _____

Numbness/tingling   _____

Feelings of unreality   _____

Feelings of choking   _____

Fear of dying   _____

Fear of losing control/going insane   _____

Thoughts: _____

Behaviors: _____

Panic Attack Record

Date: 2/16/06   Time began: 5:20 p.m.

Triggers: Home alone and shortness of breath.

Expected: ___X___   Unexpected: _____

Maximum Fear

0 ------- 1 ------- 2 ------- 3 ------- 4 ------- 5 ------- 6 ------- 7 ------- 8 ------- 9 ------- 10

  None   Mild   Moderate   Strong   Extreme

Check all symptoms present to at least a mild degree:

Symptom	
Chest pain or discomfort	_____
Sweating	___✓___
Heart racing/palpitations/pounding	___✓___
Nausea/upset stomach	_____
Shortness of breath	___✓___
Dizzy/unsteady/lightheaded/faint	_____
Shaking/trembling	___✓___
Chills/hot flushes	_____
Numbness/tingling	_____
Feelings of unreality	___✓___
Feelings of choking	_____
Fear of dying	_____
Fear of losing control/going insane	___✓___

Thoughts: I am going crazy, I will lose control.

Behaviors: Called my mother.

Figure 2.2.

Jill's Panic Attack Record (1)

Panic Attack Record

Date: 2/19/06   Time began: 3:00 a.m.

Triggers: Woke out of sleep with racing heart.

Expected: _____   Unexpected: ___X___

Maximum Fear

0 ------- 1 ------- 2 ------- 3 ------- 4 ------- 5 ------- 6 ------- 7 ------- 8 ------- 9 ------- 10

None   Mild   Moderate   Strong   Extreme

Check all symptoms present to at least a mild degree:

Chest pain or discomfort   _____

Sweating   ____✓____

Heart racing/palpitations/pounding   ____✓____

Nausea/upset stomach   _____

Shortness of breath   ____✓____

Dizzy/unsteady/lightheaded/faint   _____

Shaking/trembling   ____✓____

Chills/hot flushes   _____

Numbness/tingling   _____

Feelings of unreality   _____

Feelings of choking   _____

Fear of dying   ____✓____

Fear of losing control/going insane   _____

Thoughts: I am going to die.

Behaviors: Woke my husband.

Figure 2.3.

Jill's Panic Attack Record (2)

As shown in her second record, Jill's panic attack happened at 3:00 a.m. on February 19. This panic woke her out of sleep. In fact, the racing of her heart seemed to wake her out of sleep, so she listed racing heart as the trigger. The attack was unexpected. It took her by surprise. Her maximum fear was 7. Her symptoms included racing heart, breathing symptoms, sweating, shaking, and fears of dying. Her thoughts were that she would die, and her behavior was to wake her husband.

Anxiety and Other Moods

You can keep a record of your general feelings throughout the day as well, by completing a Daily Mood Record at the end of each day. You may photocopy the form from this book or download multiple copies at the Treatments *ThatWork*™ website (http://www.oup.com/us/ttw). Use a 10-point scale to rate your daily levels of anxiety, depression (i.e., how sad, down, or lacking in energy you are), and how much you worry about having a panic attack (i.e., how much is panic on your mind, how concerned are you with the possibility of panicking).

For all ratings, 0 = none, 5 = moderate, and 10 = extreme anxiety, depression, and worry about panic. These ratings are based on how you felt on average during the day. In other words, considering the whole day, and combining all ups and downs throughout the day together, what was your average amount of anxiety, depression, and worry about panic?

Jill's Daily Mood Record shows that over the course of the week, her patterns of anxiety, depression, and worry about panic changed. On February 16 and 17, Jill was quite worried about having a panic attack; these were the first two days after a weekend spent with her husband. Notice how she was also generally more anxious and depressed on those days compared to other days. In contrast, on February 21 and 22 (the weekend), she felt less anxious, less depressed, and less worried about panicking because her husband was with her the whole time.

Over the course of several weeks, trends often become evident. One example is the way in which moods fluctuate in relation to the frequency of panic attacks. It will be important to learn this information to make your treatment as effective as possible.

Daily Mood Record for Jill

Rate each column at the end of the day, using a number from the 0–10-point scale below.

0 ------- 1 ------- 2 ------- 3 ------- 4 ------- 5 ------- 6 ------- 7 ------- 8 ------- 9 ------- 10

| None | Mild | Moderate | Strong | Extreme |

Date	Average Anxiety	Average Depression	Average Worry About Panic
Monday 16th	7	5	7
Tuesday 17th	5	4	5
Wednesday 18th	4	4	5
Thursday 19th	4	3	4
Friday 20th	4	4	5
Saturday 21st	2	1	1
Sunday 22nd	2	2	2

Figure 2.4.

Jill's Daily Mood Record

Progress Record

The Progress Record is a chart of your progress which is divided into the number of panic attacks per week and the average level of anxiety per week. Of course, you may also record your progress in other areas as well, such as worry about panic or level of depressed mood. This Progress Record will allow you to see how you are doing and to put things into perspective. It is helpful to keep this in a visible place, such as your bathroom mirror or on the refrigerator. You may photocopy the form from this book or download multiple copies at the Treatments *ThatWork*™ website (http://www.oup.com/us/ttw).

Daily Mood Record

Rate each column at the end of the day, using a number from the 0–10-point scale below.

0 ------- 1 ------- 2 ------- 3 ------- 4 ------- 5 ------- 6 ------- 7 ------- 8 ------- 9 ------- 10

None   Mild   Moderate   Strong   Extreme

Date	Average Anxiety	Average Depression	Average Worry About Panic

Summary

We cannot emphasize enough the importance of recording. It must be done daily to get the full benefit from this program. While at first you may have to push yourself to record, it will become easier and even rewarding as time goes on. It helps to give yourself feedback, and it is also beneficial for your mental health professional if you provide this kind of information. These records will be invaluable during the rest of the program, so it is definitely worth the effort.

Progress Record

For each week, plot the number of panic attacks you experienced and your average anxiety level for that week.

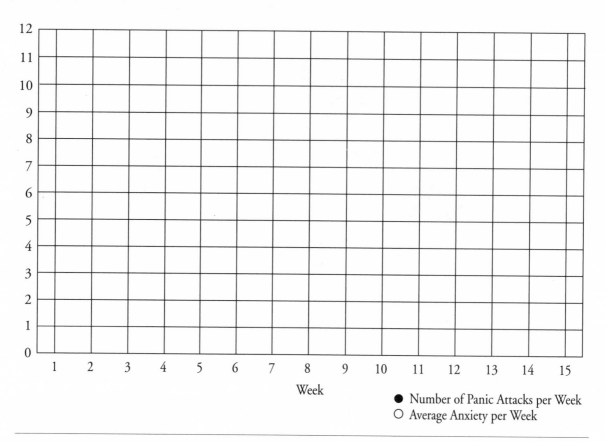

● Number of Panic Attacks per Week
○ Average Anxiety per Week

Homework

✎ Record your panic attacks and daily mood levels for at least one full week using the Panic Attack Record and Daily Mood Record.

✎ Read chapters 3 and 4 and chapter 11, section 1, over the course of the week as you record.

Self-Assessment

Answer each of the following by circling T (True) or F (False). Answers are given in the appendix.

1. Ongoing recording is important because it provides a more accurate description of fear and anxiety than do vague generalities or attempts to remember from the past.   T   F

2. Objective, matter-of-fact recording of anxiety and panic will cause more anxiety and panic attacks.   T   F

3. Recording of panic attacks is best done at the end of the day.   T   F

4. Recording helps to identify the conditions and triggers that provoke panic.   T   F

5. Recording of anxiety and other moods is done at the end of the day.   T   F

Chapter 3   *Negative Cycles of Panic and Agoraphobia*

Goals

- ■ To learn about the purpose of anxiety and panic

- ■ To learn about the parts to anxiety and panic

- ■ To discover your own thoughts, behaviors, and physical symptoms

- ■ To understand the negative cycles that contribute to panic attacks and agoraphobia

- ■ To understand how this treatment interrupts the panic and agoraphobia cycles

The Purpose of Anxiety and Panic

Anxiety and panic are natural emotional states that are experienced by everyone—it is part of the experience of being human. Anxiety is the reaction that we all have whenever we think something bad or threatening could happen. This could include physical threats, such as the possibility of illness, accident, or death; social threats, such as the possibility of embarrassment, rejection, or ridicule; or mental threats, such as the possibility of going insane, losing control, or losing one's mental faculties. The threats could be large (such as the possibility of losing one's life) or small (such as the possibility of being late for an appointment). Anxiety is our way of preparing to meet the challenge posed by these threats. It helps to gear us up and protect us from whatever is threatening.

Anxiety is not bad in and of itself, and it can be a productive, driving force. Years of research have shown that having some anxiety enhances performance. That is, you do better at what you are doing, whether in the classroom or on the job, when anxiety is present up to a certain level. Imagine absolutely no anxiety about a job interview—you would be less motivated to put your best foot forward to meet the challenge of getting the job. However, anxiety can vary in severity, from mild uneasiness to extreme dis-

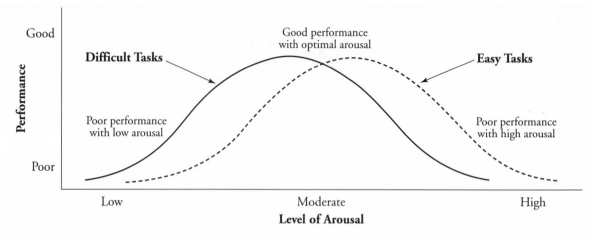

Figure 3.1.

Yerkes-Dodson Law

tress. At the extreme end, anxiety can interfere with what you are doing. Imagine extreme anxiety in a job interview which leads to poor concentration and stammering. The notion that some anxiety is helpful for learning and performance, whereas too much anxiety can interfere with learning and performance, is shown above in the standard diagram of the Yerkes-Dodson Law.

Anxiety can vary in frequency, from occasional episodes to seemingly constant unease. When anxiety is very frequent, it can interfere with daily life. The goals of this program are to decrease the likelihood of becoming anxious unnecessarily and to decrease the intensity of anxiety so that you can function normally. The goal, however, is not to remove anxiety altogether.

How does this discussion relate to panic disorder? In the case of panic disorder, anxiety is experienced because of the "threat" of panic. As described in more detail in the next chapter, panic is regarded as threatening because of beliefs that panic could cause you to die, lose control, or go insane. As you will see, these beliefs are incorrect. Anxiety about the threat of panicking is unnecessary because panic attacks actually are not harmful.

The Parts to Anxiety and Panic

There are three major parts to panic and anxiety: physical symptoms, thoughts, and behaviors. The physical part involves the symptoms of rapid heartbeat, difficulty breathing, nervous stomach, diarrhea, sweating, shaking, headaches, stomachaches, a lump in the throat, frequent urination, fatigue, restlessness, visual disturbances, a sense of pressure in the head, and many more. The physical symptoms can be acute, lasting a short period of time (as in panic attacks), or can be prolonged, lasting hours or days (as in general anxiety). Also, the acute physical symptoms can shift from one panic attack to the next. On one occasion, you may notice strong symptoms of shortness of breath, while on another occasion you may instead notice a racing and pounding heart.

The thoughts are beliefs, or things that we say to ourselves, or images of impending doom or of something terrible that is about to happen. We refer to these as *negative thoughts*. Most often, thoughts during panic attacks are about *immediate* physical catastrophes (such as fainting, dying, heart attack, brain tumor), social catastrophes (such as ridicule or jeering), or mental catastrophes (such as going insane or losing control). Thoughts during anxiety are about bad things that could happen *in the future,* such as job loss or the worst panic attack ever.

The behaviors are things we do, such as pacing up and down, fidgeting, or escaping from or avoiding places where anxiety and panic are expected to occur. An example of escaping is to leave a shopping mall as soon as feelings of anxiety or panic develop. An example of avoiding is to not enter a shopping mall at all because of concerns about panicking once inside. Other behaviors include looking for exits or ways out of situations, relying on objects that make you feel better (these are the superstitious objects we described in chapter 1), or seeking help (such as at medical centers).

These three parts often differ from times when you are anxious to times when you panic. Thoughts during anxiety usually have to do with the future (e.g., "My boss could give me a negative evaluation at the end of the year," or, "It would be horrible if I panicked at the party tomorrow"), whereas thoughts during panic attacks are usually about the immediate situation (e.g., "I am going to faint right now," or, "I must be crazy"). Also, anxious behaviors include avoiding situations or extra cautiousness (such as mapping out directions fully in advance), whereas behaviors during panic have more to do with escaping or finding help. Finally, physical symptoms during anxiety usually are long lasting and involve muscle tension, restlessness, and fatigue; whereas panic attack symptoms are more abrupt and tend to decrease more quickly than the physical symptoms of anxiety, and include heart palpitations, shortness of breath, and other symptoms listed in the table in chapter 1.

Think about your own thoughts, symptoms, and behaviors when you are in the midst of a panic attack, and consider your own thoughts, symptoms, and behaviors when you are generally anxious (such as when you are worrying about having a panic attack in the future).

Remember Jill? During her panic attacks, her most common symptoms were a racing heart, shortness of breath, and feelings of unreality and numbness; her most common thoughts were that she would lose control or go insane; and her most common behaviors were to leave wherever she was and find either her husband or her mother. In contrast, when she worried about panic attacks in the future, her thoughts varied based on whatever she was worrying about; her most common symptoms were an upset stomach, muscle tension, and fatigue; and her most common behaviors consisted of biting her nails and seeking reassurance from her husband that everything would be okay.

On the Parts of Panic and the Parts of Anxiety forms provided on pages 45 and 46, record what you typically think, what you physically feel, and what you do when you panic and when you feel anxious. You may photocopy these forms from the book or download multiple copies at the Treatments *ThatWork*™ website (http://www.oup.com/us/ttw).

The Panic Cycle

Physical symptoms, thoughts, and behaviors contribute to each other in what is called a *negative cycle*. In other words, they tend to snowball off each other. For example, negative thoughts can directly increase physical symptoms. If we tell ourselves that something dangerous is about to occur (e.g., "I am about to have a heart attack"), then physical tension will increase because our bodies pump out more adrenalin and operate at faster rates whenever we face danger. In turn, a physical symptom, such as a racing heart, may lead to more negative thoughts. This is particularly likely if you believe that normal symptoms of tension are dangerous (e.g., "The fact that my heart rate has not slowed down must surely mean that something is terribly wrong"). Behaviors of fidgeting, pacing, and escaping a situation can increase levels of physical tension as well because of the physical effort they involve.

Parts of Panic

Physical Symptoms

1. _____

2. _____

3. _____

Thoughts

1. _____

_____

_____

2. _____

_____

_____

3. _____

_____

_____

Behaviors

1. _____

_____

_____

2. _____

_____

_____

3. _____

_____

_____

Parts of Anxiety

Physical Symptoms

1. _____

2. _____

3. _____

Thoughts

1. _____

_____

_____

2. _____

_____

_____

3. _____

_____

_____

Behaviors

1. _____

_____

_____

2. _____

_____

_____

3. _____

_____

_____

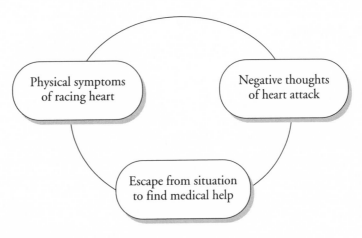

Figure 3.2.

The Panic Cycle

More specifically, the thought that a racing heart is a sign of heart disease is frightening and will produce more raciness of the heart. In turn, the continued raciness may lead to stronger beliefs that something is terribly wrong with the heart. It may also lead to attempts to get medical help. Such negative thoughts and behaviors may again prolong the racing of the heart. In other words, negative thoughts lead to fear, and fear leads to more physical symptoms and escape behaviors that snowball into more negative thoughts, and so on. The end result is intense fear or panic, as is shown in Figure 3.2. This is called a *panic cycle*. Another example is to think that shortness of breath means that you are about to suffocate. That thought will cause more physical tension and more symptoms of shortness of breath, as well as attempts to breath more deeply, which in turn may contribute to shortness of breath (for reasons described later), and so on.

In contrast, thinking that a racing heart is harmless and not reason for concern will interrupt this negative cycle, with the end result that panic does not occur. This is shown in Figure 3.3. Similarly, realizing that shortness of breath is not a sign of impending suffocation will offset the chances of a panic attack.

Think about a recent panic attack and the physical symptoms, negative thoughts and behaviors, and the ways in which they contributed to each other. What was the first thing that happened? Was it a physical symptom or a thought? What happened next? Did your physical symptoms increase, and what did that lead you to think? How did you behave? How did your reactions influence your physical symptoms? An example of this kind of step-by-step analysis is provided in the next section.

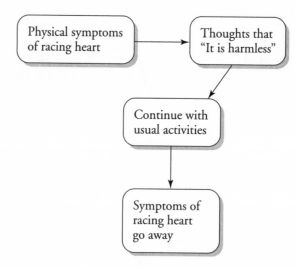

Figure 3.3.
Interruption to Panic Cycle

Case Studies: Step-by-Step Analysis

■ *The very first thing I felt was when I stood up—my head started to feel really weird, as if it was spinning inside [physical symptom]. My reaction was to hold onto the chair [behavior]. I thought something was wrong [negative thought]. I thought it could get worse and worse and that I would faint and collapse [negative thought]. By then, I was feeling very nervous. As the dizziness got worse and worse [physical symptom], I became really concerned, because it was different from any other experience I had ever had. I was convinced that this was "it"—that I was going to collapse and that nobody would find me [negative thought]. That's when I called my husband [behavior] and waited for him to arrive [behavior].* ■

Here is another example.

■ *I was sitting in front of the television watching ER. They were showing a scene of someone dying from a heart attack. I felt a slight pain in my chest [physical symptom] and immediately started to wonder if something was wrong—maybe I was having a heart attack [negative thought]. My heart began to pound and speed up [physical symptom], and I became very nervous. My breathing was faster [physical symptom]. I took my pulse and started to walk around to distract myself [behaviors]. But my heart rate was still going fast, and I felt like I couldn't get a deep breath of air [physical feelings]. I was sure that I was going to collapse at any moment [negative thought]. I thought of calling 911 but decided to just sit by the phone for a while [behavior], and then eventually, the feelings passed.* ■

Use the Step-by-Step Panic Analysis of Panic Attack form (on page 50) to understand one of your own recent panic attacks. You may photocopy the form from this book or download multiple copies from the Treatments *ThatWork*™ website (http://www.oup.com/us/ttw).

By understanding these cycles (from negative thoughts, to physical symptoms, to behaviors, to more negative thoughts and more physical symptoms, and so on), you will develop a good awareness of what causes panic attacks. These records will also help you to understand that the way to interrupt these cycles is to change the way you think about and respond to physical symptoms.

Agoraphobia Cycle

If you are anxious about physical symptoms, it is likely that you are especially watchful for those symptoms as you enter a situation from which escape is not easy or in which help is not available. For example, you might be particularly attentive to dizziness as you drive on an unfamiliar road. If you become afraid of the symptom in that situation, then it is understandable how you might feel panicky or that you would attempt to find an exit. However, by escaping the situation, you may feel even more anxiety the next time you attempt to enter that situation, and you may feel even less likely to enter the situation in the future. That is, the fear has been reinforced because you did not learn that it was safe to continue in the situation, despite the physical symptoms. This sequence of events is shown in Figure 3.4.

Interrupting Panic and Agoraphobia Cycles

This program teaches you ways of interrupting the panic and agoraphobia cycles. It consists of strategies to help you think differently about and to behave differently toward physical symptoms. It teaches you how to no longer be panicked by physical symptoms and to no longer avoid physical symptoms or the situations in which they are expected to occur.

Step-by-Step Analysis of Panic Attack

Where were you and what was going on when the panic attack first started? _____

_____

_____

_____

What happened first? A physical symptom, negative thought, or a behavior? _____

_____

_____

What happened next? How did you react to the first physical symptom or negative thought? Did you notice more physical symptoms, more negative thoughts, or did you do something, such as seek help, lie down, or exit wherever you were?

_____

_____

_____

What happened next? Did the physical symptoms get worse, did you become even more scared about negative things happening?

_____

_____

_____

What was next? _____

_____

_____

_____

How did it end? _____

_____

_____

_____

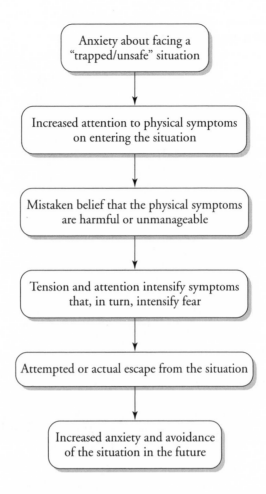

Figure 3.4.

The Agoraphobia Cycle

You will be taught two coping skills. The first strategy is breathing skills. Breathing skills are designed to regulate breathing and interrupt the panic and agoraphobia cycles by providing a tool for you to continue in whatever activity you are engaging and face your fear rather than avoid it. The second coping skill is directed at your negative thoughts. Once you are able to discover exactly what negative thoughts you have, you will learn to treat them as guesses rather than facts. You will develop alternative ways of thinking that are more based on evidence than conjecture.

You will use these two coping skills to help deal with the situations that you have been avoiding because of anticipation of panic attacks (i.e, agoraphobia). You will learn to be less afraid of these situations and to realize that they are harmless. In addition, you will use the coping skills to deal directly with physical symptoms that make you anxious, such as shortness of breath, dizziness, or palpitations. You will learn to be less afraid of those symptoms and to realize that they are harmless. You will learn how to deal directly with the physical symptoms when they occur in agoraphobia situations. Everything you learn in this treatment must be put into practice over and over again until it becomes part of your natural method of responding.

Homework

🖎 Continue to record your anxiety and panic for one week using the Panic Attack Record and the Daily Mood Record.

🖎 Read chapter 4 and chapter 11, section 1, over the course of the week of recording.

Self-Assessment

Answer each of the following by circling T (True) or F (False). Answers are given in the appendix.

1. Anxiety and panic are made up of three main parts: physical symptoms, negative thoughts, and behaviors.   T   F

2. One should never feel anxious.   T   F

3. What you think has absolutely no effect on what you feel physically.   T   F

4. Panic attacks just hit you—there is no reason for them.   T   F

5. Anxiety is usually in anticipation of future dangers, whereas panic is a sudden rush of fear in response to immediate dangers.   T   F

6. The treatment program presented in this workbook involves positive thinking, meditating, and chilling out.   T   F

7. Avoidance of an agoraphobia situation has no long-term negative effect.   T   F

Chapter 4

Panic Attacks Are Not Harmful

Goals

- ◼ To learn about the causes of the physical symptoms of panic
- ◼ To learn that the physical symptoms of panic are not harmful
- ◼ To understand why panic attacks seem to come from "out of the blue"

Physical Symptoms of Panic and Survival of the Fittest

Because negative thoughts contribute to panic, and because the negative thoughts often have to do with believing that the physical symptoms are harmful, it is important to have an accurate understanding of the physical symptoms of panic. This information will help you realize that the physical symptoms of panic are *not* harmful.

Scientifically, immediate or short-term fear (i.e., a panic attack) is named the *fight-flight response.* The effects of this response are aimed toward either fighting with or fleeing from danger. The number-one purpose of panic is to protect us from danger. When our ancestors lived in caves, it was vital that when faced with danger, an automatic response would take over, causing them to take immediate action (attack or run). Even in today's hectic world, this is a necessary mechanism. Just imagine if you were crossing a street when suddenly a car sped toward you blasting its horn. If you experienced absolutely no fear, you would be killed. What actually happens is that your fight-flight response takes over, and you run out of the way. The purpose of panic is to protect us, not to harm us. It is our survival mechanism, and it involves the following physical changes in our bodies.

Nervous and Chemical Effects

When danger is detected, the brain sends messages to a section of your nerves called the *autonomic nervous system.* The autonomic nervous system has two subsections, or branches, called the *sympathetic nervous system* and the *parasympathetic nervous system.* These two branches of the nervous system are directly involved in controlling your body's energy levels and its preparation for action. The sympathetic nervous system is the fight-flight system, which releases energy and gets the body ready for action (fighting or fleeing). The parasympathetic nervous system is the restoring system, which returns the body to a normal state. Activation of the sympathetic nervous system is believed to cause most panic attack symptoms.

The sympathetic nervous system tends to be an all-or-none system. When it is activated, all of its parts respond. This may explain why most panic attacks involve many physical symptoms and not just one or two. In addition, the sympathetic nervous system responds immediately, as soon as danger is close at hand (e.g., think of the rush that you experience when you think another car on the freeway is about to hit you). That is why the physical symptoms of panic attacks can occur almost instantaneously, within seconds.

The sympathetic nervous system releases two chemicals, *adrenalin* and *noradrenalin,* from the adrenal glands on the kidneys. These chemicals are used as messengers by the sympathetic nervous system to continue activity so that once activity begins, it often continues and increases for some time. However, the sympathetic nervous system activity is stopped in two ways. First, the chemical messengers adrenalin and noradrenalin are eventually destroyed by other chemicals in the body. Second, the parasympathetic nervous system (which generally has opposing effects to the sympathetic nervous system) becomes activated and restores a relaxed feeling. Eventually, the body will "have enough" of the fight-flight response, and the parasympathetic nervous system will restore a relaxed feeling. In other words, panic can neither continue forever nor spiral to ever-increasing and damaging levels. The parasympathetic nervous system stops the sympathetic nervous system from getting "carried away."

Adrenalin and noradrenalin take some time to be fully destroyed. Even after your sympathetic nervous system has stopped responding, you are likely to feel "keyed up" or "on edge" for some time because the chemicals are still floating around in your system. This is perfectly natural and harmless. In fact, there is a purpose to this—in the wild, danger often has a habit of returning. So, it is useful for us to remain in a "keyed-up" state so that we can quickly reactivate the fight-flight response if danger returns.

Each physical effect of the fight-flight system is intended to prepare you to fight or flee—that is, to protect you. The fight-flight system affects our hearts, blood flow, breathing, sweating, pupils, muscles, and digestive system, as well as other parts of our body.

Cardiovascular Effects

Activity in the sympathetic nervous system increases heart rate and the strength of the heartbeat. This is vital to preparation for action (to fight or flee) because it speeds up the blood flow, improving delivery of oxygen to the tissues and removal of waste products from the tissues. The muscle tissues need oxygen as a source of energy for fighting or fleeing. This is why a racing or pounding heart is typically experienced during periods of high anxiety or panic.

Also, there is a change in the blood flow. Basically, blood is taken away from the places where it is not needed (by a tightening of the blood vessels) and is directed toward the places where it is needed more (by an expansion of the blood vessels). For example, blood is taken away from the skin, fingers, and toes. This is useful because, thinking back to our ancestral cave days, the extremities are the most likely place to be attacked and injured. Having less blood flow there means that we are less likely to bleed to death. As a result, the skin looks pale and feels cold, especially around the hands and feet. Instead, the blood goes to the large muscles, such as the thighs, heart, and biceps, which need the oxygen for fighting or fleeing. The big muscles are most important for running or fighting.

Together, these physical changes cause the heart to race or pound and the skin to feel pale and cold, especially around the toes and fingers, sometimes causing feelings of weakness in the hands and feet. You might feel cold even though it is a warm day. These are normal physical feelings under conditions of being afraid or anxious. It is a sign that the body is preparing to take action.

Sometimes, people report feeling hot instead of cold. Hot feelings are more likely to occur during the abrupt rush of panic, as soon as the sympathetic nervous system is activated and before the blood flow is redirected. The cold chills that go along with the redirection of the blood flow are more likely to occur with slow-building or longer-lasting anxiety.

Respiration Effects

Another effect is for breathing to become faster and deeper, because the body needs more oxygen to be able to fight or flee. Sometimes, breathing can become unbalanced and cause harmless but unpleasant symptoms such as breathlessness, choking or smothering feelings, and pain or tightness in the chest. Also, the blood supply to the head may be decreased. While this is only a small amount and is not at all dangerous, it produces unpleasant (but harmless) symptoms, including dizziness, blurred vision, confusion, feelings of unreality (or, feeling as if you are in a dream state), and hot flushes. These physical symptoms might be uncomfortable but are not at all harmful and are not a sign that something is seriously wrong with you.

Sweat-Gland Effects

The fight-flight response increases sweating. Sweating cools the body to prevent it from overheating and allows you to continue fighting or fleeing from danger without collapsing from heat. In addition, excessive sweating makes the skin slippery, so that it is more difficult for a predator to grasp. Perspiration is a common symptom of anxiety and panic.

Other Physical Effects

Also, the pupils (the center of the eyes) widen to let in more light. This helps us to scan the environment for whatever is dangerous. Remember, panic and anxiety are reactions to the perception of threat, and if a threat or danger is expected to occur, then it makes sense for us to be on guard and looking for it by increasing our field of vision. At the same time, the change in the pupils may cause symptoms such as blurred vision, spots in front of the eyes, or sensitivity to bright lights.

Another physical effect is a decrease in salivation, resulting in a dry mouth. In fact, the whole digestive system is decreased, so that energy that is required for food digestion can be redirected to the muscles that are needed to fight or flee. This often causes nausea, heavy feelings in the stomach, and sometimes diarrhea as material that could "weigh us down" while attempting to fight or flee is evacuated from the body.

Also, many of the muscle groups tense up in preparation for fight or flight, and this results in feelings of tension. This tension can sometimes cause aches and pains, as well as trembling and shaking. Another interesting effect is the release of natural analgesics (i.e., painkillers) from the brain, so that we are less likely to feel pain when we are afraid. The purpose of this is to enable you to continue fighting or fleeing from danger even if you have been injured. Connected with this is the release of coagulants and lymphocytes into the blood which helps to seal wounds and repair tissue damage. In addition, there is a contraction of the spleen, so that more red blood cells are released to carry more oxygen around the blood, and there is a release of stored sugar from the liver, so that the muscles have more sugar available as a source of energy.

Finally, because the fight-flight response produces a general activation of the whole body, and because this takes a lot of energy, people generally feel tired, drained, and "washed out" afterward.

In summary, the physical changes that underlie the physical symptoms of panic and anxiety are protective in that they are designed to help us escape from or fight off danger. The symptoms are real, but they are not harmful. Interestingly, physical symptoms are sometimes felt in the absence of actual physical changes. For example, sometimes people feel as if the heart is racing when, in fact, it is beating at a normal pace. Or, sometimes people feel hot, even though their skin temperature has not changed. This occurs because an intense and anxious focus on physical feelings can create the perception of a physical disturbance even when none really exists. However, intense panic attacks are almost always based on real physical changes. These are summarized in Table 4.1.

How Do Physical Symptoms Influence What We Think and Do?

When the sympathetic nervous system is activated into an emergency fight-flight response, there are certain natural effects on our behaviors and our thoughts. (Remember, anxiety and panic are made up of physical symptoms, thoughts, and behaviors.)

Table 4.1. Physiology of Fear

Physical Change	Purpose	Symptom
Increased heart rate and strength of heartbeat.	Speed up delivery of oxygen and removal of carbon dioxide.	Racing or pounding heart.
Redirection of blood flow away from skin, toes, and fingers and toward the big muscles.	Provide the big muscles with energy for fight-flight response, lose less blood if attacked.	Pale and cold, especially in hands and feet.
Increased rate and depth of breathing.	Provide more oxygen for muscles as energy for fight-flight response.	Fast breathing. Also, dizziness, lightheadedness, shortness of breath, feelings of hot or cold, sweating, chest discomfort, visual changes, if the increased oxygen is not used.
Increased activity in sweat glands.	Cool body to prevent exhaustion from overheating.	Sweating.
Pupils (eyes) dilate.	Increase visual field to scan for danger.	Eyes more sensitive to light.
Less energy to digestive system.	Direct all energy toward fight-flight response.	Dry mouth, nausea, stomachache, cramps, diarrhea.
Increased muscle readiness.	Preparation for fight-flight response.	Muscle tension, muscle cramps, trembling, shaking.
Release of natural pain killers (opioids).	Dulls pain sensitivity to allow continued fighting or fleeing if injured.	Less sensitive to pain.

The Behavior of Fight-Flight Response

The emergency fight-flight response prepares the body to either attack or run. It is no surprise that the overwhelming urge to escape is associated with panic. Sometimes, escape is not possible, such as when you are in church in the middle of the pew or at an important meeting. At these times, the urge to escape may become stronger or be shown through such behaviors as foot tapping, pacing, or snapping at people.

The Thoughts of Fight-Flight

The number-one effect of the emergency fight-flight response on our thinking is to alert us to the possibility of danger. One of the major effects is an immediate shift in attention to search for a potential threat—we stop attending to ongoing chores and scan our surroundings for danger.

It is understandable to have the fight-flight response if we are attacked, trapped in an elevator, or experiencing any other major stress. But why does the fight-flight response occur where there is nothing to be frightened of, when there is no obvious danger? Remember, a panic attack is a normal bodily response to fear. What makes it abnormal is when it occurs at the wrong time, when there is no real danger.

It appears that people with panic attacks are frightened of the physical symptoms of fear. Panic attacks represent "anxiety about fear." A panic attack follows a typical sequence. First, unexpected physical symptoms are experienced. (They are unexpected because they cannot be explained by any real danger at that moment.) Second, those physical symptoms provoke anxiety and fear.

Reasons for Unexpected Physical Symptoms

Why do you have the physical symptoms in the first place? There are many possible reasons for this. One is stress, including stress from work pressures, rushing to appointments, relationships, and so forth, which leads to an increase in the production of adrenalin and other stress-related chemicals. This is your body's way of staying alert and prepared to deal with the stress. However, these stress effects will cause physical symptoms.

A second reason is being anxious about having another panic attack. Anxious anticipation of anything contributes to higher levels of physical tension and more physical symptoms of stress. Also, anxiety causes us to focus our attention on whatever it is that we are anxious about. For example, anticipating social rejection leads to an intense focus on facial expressions as we look for signs of rejection. In the case of anxiety about panic, this means that attention becomes focused on physical symptoms. You may find yourself scanning your body for unusual physical symptoms and detecting symptoms that you might not have otherwise noticed. Anxiety about having panic attacks causes more symptoms of panic and more attention to those symptoms. Consequently, anxiety about panic causes more of the very things (i.e., the physical symptoms) that the person with panic disorder is afraid of and, therefore, more panic attacks.

A third reason is that normal physical symptoms happen to everyone, because our bodies are constantly changing: heart rate, skin temperature, and blood flow fluctuate greatly throughout the typical 24-hour day.

Effects of Being Afraid of Physical Symptoms

As discussed earlier, the emergency fight-flight response causes the brain to search for danger. Sometimes, an obvious threat cannot be found, as is usually the case for panic attacks that seem to occur for no reason. However, most of us cannot accept having no explanation. When an explanation cannot be found, the search may be turned inward. In other words, "if there is nothing to explain my feelings of panic and anxiety, then there must be something wrong with me." Then, the brain invents an explanation, such as: "I must be dying, losing control, or going insane." As we have seen, nothing could be further from the truth, since the purpose of the fight-flight response is to protect and not to harm us.

These types of negative thoughts about the physical symptoms of panic only contribute in a negative cycle to more negative thoughts, physical symptoms, and behaviors of panic. This was described in chapter 3 as the *panic cycle.* The negative thoughts intensify the fight-flight response because the body reacts with an impulse to fight or flee when danger (in this case, the possibilities of dying, losing control, or going insane) arises. This is true even if the danger is based on a perception of what could happen—it does not have to be a real danger. As long as we think that we are in danger, our bodies will react accordingly. As a result, the very thing that is feared (i.e., the physical symptom) is intensified. That is, a physical symptom is experienced, the physical symptom is feared (because it is judged to be dangerous), and as a result, the physical symptom intensifies. This lasts until the cycle is ended by either physical compensations, which slow everything down (i.e., *parasympathetic activation*), or by realizing that you no longer need to be afraid of the physical symptom.

In summary, physical symptoms are feared because of beliefs that they are signs of impending death, insanity, loss of control, embarrassment, and so on. In turn, these beliefs generate fear, more physical symptoms, and a snowball of anxiety and panic.

After a number of times of being afraid of physical symptoms, the fear of physical symptoms can occur "automatically." The "automatic" quality is typical of much of what we learn. Think of when you first learned to ride a bike or to drive a car. Initially, it took a lot of concentration and self-instruction about what to do each step of the way. Gradually, it became automatic, so that you could ride and drive without consciously thinking about what you were doing. And yet, your automatic thoughts are still guiding the behavior of how to drive. The same thing happens with the negative thoughts associated with panic and anxiety. Over time, they can become automatic, so that you are not aware of what you are thinking; and yet, those thoughts still influence your feelings and behaviors. Because you are not aware of your thoughts, it might feel like panic and anxiety comes from "out of the blue"—you just feel afraid, and you do not know why.

Another automatic process is called *interoceptive conditioning*. This means learning to be afraid of physical symptoms because of prior negative experiences in association with those symptoms. For example, imagine that you were violently ill every time you noticed a muscle spasm in your leg. Pretty soon, you would learn to be afraid of muscle spasms in your leg in anticipation of being violently ill. The same thing happens with panic; but in this case, the muscle spasm is a physical symptom that happens during panic (such as a racing heart), and the violent illness is the terror caused by beliefs that you might die, lose control, or go insane. Once the possibility of death or some other catastrophe is linked to a racing heart, changes in heart rate can cause automatic fear since the fear is conditioned. Consequently, even minor changes in heart rate that are normal, and did not bother you before you experienced panic, can cause you to become afraid. In fact, the physical change may be so subtle that you are not fully aware of it, and yet it still causes you to be afraid. This is another reason why panic attacks sometimes feel as if they come from out of the blue—they are actually being triggered by subtle physical changes of which you are not consciously aware but to which your body has become conditioned to react.

When judgments about the physical symptoms being dangerous occur automatically (or, without conscious awareness), or when the fear is conditioned to physical symptoms of even the slightest intensity so that you are not aware of what you are responding to, then panic attacks seem to occur from nowhere. Also, remember that our fight-flight emergency response systems are designed in such a way as to respond instantaneously. Without such a capacity for instantaneous response, we would not be able to survive, because dangers can sometimes come at us very quickly. The consequence in terms of panic attacks is that automatic beliefs and conditioning can happen so quickly that the end result—the panic attack—seems as if it happened without time for thought or reaction. However, in reality, our fear is always triggered by something. That is, the physical symptoms, or the negative thoughts about physical symptoms, are always present, even if not immediately obvious.

This is even true for panic attacks that occur from a relaxed state and for panic attacks that wake you up out of deep sleep (i.e., *nocturnal panic attacks*). During relaxation, physical feelings are often different from normal, sometimes resulting in feelings of floating or being in a trance. If you are afraid of physical feelings that are different from normal, then the physical feelings you have during relaxation could trigger a panic attack. Nocturnal panic attacks are experienced by about one half of the people who suffer from panic disorder. About 25% have repeated panic attacks out of sleep. You might ask, "How can nocturnal panic attacks be triggered by physical feelings"? First, it is normal to have changes in physical rhythms during sleep. For example, heart rates and breathing rates increase and decrease at different times throughout the night. Second, we have the capacity to respond to meaningful events throughout our sleep. Think of the mother of a newborn child who wakes in response to the slightest sound from her baby while sleeping through other, louder sounds. Another example would be soldiers in combat who have the capacity to sleep through the sound of allied planes but wake to the sound of enemy planes. Thus, if physical changes are meaningful (in other words, if they are frightening), it is understandable that physical changes that normally happen throughout sleep could cause someone to wake out of sleep in a panic attack, in the same way that panic attacks happen during the day. This is especially likely to happen if the physical changes happen at a time throughout sleep when it is easier to be woken. For example, it is very hard to be woken out of deep sleep and out of rapid eye movement (REM) sleep, but it is easier to be woken out of Stages 2 and 3 of sleep.

Thus, a simplified model of panic attacks looks like the depiction in Figure 4.1.

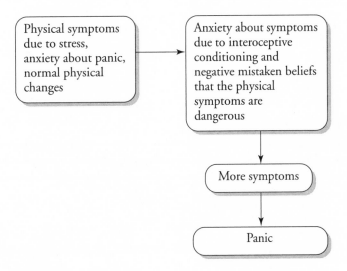

Figure 4.1.

A Simplified Model of Panic Attacks

In summary, panic is based on the fight-flight response, in which the primary purpose is to activate the organism and protect it from harm. Everyone is capable of this response when confronted with danger, whether that danger is real or imagined. Associated with this response are a number of physical symptoms, behaviors, and thoughts. When physical symptoms occur in the absence of an obvious explanation, people often misinterpret the normal emergency symptoms as indicating a serious physical or mental problem. In this case, the physical symptoms themselves can become threatening and can trigger the fight-flight response again.

Typical Mistaken Beliefs About Panic Symptoms

As noted, when physical symptoms occur without an obvious explanation, we tend to search inwardly for an explanation; and in so doing, sometimes the normal symptoms of fear are misunderstood as a serious physical or mental problem. Such mistaken beliefs can result in a vicious "fear of fear" cycle. Common myths and mistaken beliefs about the physical symptoms of fear include sensations of going insane, losing control, suffering nervous collapse, suffering a heart attack, and fainting. Let us now evaluate each of these.

Going Insane

Many people believe that the physical symptoms of fear or panic mean they are going insane. They are most likely referring to the severe mental disorder known as *schizophrenia*. Let us look at schizophrenia to see how likely this is. Schizophrenia is a major disorder characterized by such severe symptoms as disjointed thoughts and speech (such as rapid shifting from one topic to the next), sometimes extending to speech that does not make any sense; delusions or strange beliefs; and hallucinations. An example of a strange belief might be the perception of receiving of messages from outer space, and an example of a hallucination might be hearing a conversation when there is no one around.

Schizophrenia generally begins very gradually and not suddenly, such as during a panic attack. Also, because this illness runs in families and has a strong genetic base, only a certain proportion of people can become schizophrenic, and in other people, no amount of stress will cause the disorder. In addition, people who become schizophrenic usually show some mild symptoms for most of their lives (such as unusual thoughts). If this has not been noticed yet in you, then the chances are that you will not become schizophrenic. This is especially true if you are over 25 years of age, because schizophrenia generally first appears in the late teens to early 20s. Finally, if you have been through interviews with a psychologist or psychiatrist, then you can be fairly certain that they would have told you if you have schizophrenia.

Losing Control

Some people believe they are going to "lose control" when they panic. They usually mean that they will become totally paralyzed and not able to move or that they will not know what they are doing and will run around wildly, hurting people, yelling out obscenities, and generally embarrassing themselves. Or, they may not know what to expect but may just experience an overwhelming feeling of being out of control.

Even though panic attacks can make you feel somewhat confused and unreal, you are still able to think and function. In fact, you are probably able to think faster, and you are actually physically stronger, and your reflexes are quicker. The same kind of thing happens when people are in real emergencies—

think of mothers and fathers who accomplish amazing things (such as lifting extremely heavy objects) and overcome their own intense fears in order to save their children.

Sometimes, the strong urge to escape is misunderstood as losing control. For example, a patient at our clinic was driving to a job interview when she panicked, changed direction, and headed for her husband's office instead. She believed that this was a loss of control. On the contrary, she was in complete control since she was doing whatever she thought was necessary to get to safety. Given her fears (she thought she was going to die), getting to her husband was a natural thing for her to do. Most people would do the same if they believed that they were about to die. So, the behavior was controlled. The problem was her mistaken belief that she was dying.

Nervous Collapse

Many people believe that their nerves might become exhausted and that they may thus collapse. However, this is not at all likely. As discussed earlier, panic is based on activity in the sympathetic nervous system which is then counteracted by the parasympathetic nervous system. The parasympathetic nervous system is, in a sense, a safeguard to protect against the possibility that the sympathetic nervous system may become "worn out." Nerves are not like electrical wires, and anxiety cannot wear out, damage, or use up nerves, although continuous anxiety may make you more sensitive to negative events.

Heart Attacks

Many people misunderstand the symptoms of panic as signs of a heart attack. This is probably because they lack knowledge about heart attacks. Let us look at the facts of heart disease and see how this differs from panic attacks. The major symptoms of heart disease are breathlessness and chest pain, as well as occasional palpitations and fainting. The symptoms in heart disease are generally directly related to effort. That is, the harder you exercise, the worse the symptoms, and the less you exercise, the better the symptoms. The symptoms usually go away fairly quickly with rest. This is very different from the symptoms of panic attacks, which often occur at rest and seem to have a mind of their own. Certainly, panic symptoms can happen and even intensify during exercise. However, this is different from the symptoms of a heart attack, because panic symptoms occur equally often at rest. Of most importance is the fact that heart disease will almost always produce major electrical changes in the heart which can be detected by an electrocardiogram (EKG) recording. In panic attacks, the only change that shows up on an EKG is an increase in heart rate. In and of itself, increased heart rate is not at all dangerous, unless it reaches extremely high rates, such as over 200 beats per minute, for prolonged periods, which far exceed the rates that occur during panic attacks. A typical heart rate during a strong panic attack is around 120–130 beats per minute. Vigorous physical exercise increases heart rate to around 150–180 beats per minute, depending on your age and fitness level. The usual heart rate when resting is anywhere from 60 to 85 beats per minute. Thus, if you have had an EKG and the doctor has given you the all clear, you can safely assume that heart disease is not the reason for your panic attacks and that panic attacks will not lead to heart disease.

Fainting

Fear of fainting is common in people with panic disorder, but actual fainting is very rare. The fear of fainting is usually based on the mistaken belief that symptoms such as dizziness and lightheadedness mean that one is about to faint. In fact, the state of panic is incompatible with fainting. The physical tension (sympathetic nervous system activation) of panic attacks is the direct opposite of what happens during fainting. Fainting is most likely to happen to people who have low blood pressure or who respond to stress with major reductions in blood pressure.

Other common myths or mistaken beliefs about panic symptoms include the ideas that they may lead to an aneurysm, an epileptic attack, or to death from shock.

Where Do Mistaken Beliefs Come From?

Information given to you from other people about the dangers of physical symptoms can be a very powerful agent for developing mistaken beliefs. For example, we have come across a dictionary definition of panic (in a reputable medical guide) as a state that can lead into psychotic depression.

That is misinformation, as there is no evidence to suggest that panic leads to psychosis. However, for someone without a background in psychological research, that kind of information could easily provide the basis for a fear of becoming psychotic during panic attacks. If someone is afraid of becoming psychotic, then it is understandable that the experience of panic is terrifying, leading to anxiety about the next panic attack.

Observing others be afraid of physical symptoms is another way in which one may develop mistaken beliefs. For example, children who observe their mother or father show excessive concern over health issues are probably more likely to develop mistaken beliefs about their own bodily symptoms.

Finally, traumatic events that you have personally experienced may contribute to mistaken beliefs that physical symptoms are harmful. For example, surgeries (especially ones that did not go smoothly in the recovery phase), dangerous allergic reactions to drugs, or serious physical illnesses may contribute to tendencies to view physical feelings with caution.

Homework

✎ Continue to record your anxiety and panic for one week, using the Panic Attack Records and Daily Mood Record.

✎ Read chapter 11, section 1, over the course of the week.

✎ Continue on to chapter 5 once you have completed at least one week of recording your panic attacks and moods and have read chapters 2–4 and chapter 11, section 1.

Self-Assessment

Answer each of the following by circling T (True) or F (False). Answers are given in the appendix.

1. A panic attack is a medical problem over which you have no control.   T   F

2. The symptoms experienced during panic, such as racing heart and sweating, are indicative of a medical disease.   T   F

3. Panic involves activation of the fight-flight response, which is intended to protect you from harm. T   F

4. Panic attacks that seem to occur from "out of the blue" often can be related to subtle physical changes, such as those caused by changes in breathing or by excitement from other events. T   F

5. A panic reaction could go on forever. T   F

6. People do not go insane when they panic. T   F

Chapter 5

Establishing Your Hierarchy of Agoraphobia Situations

Goals

■ Review information from recording panic attacks and moods

■ Develop a hierarchy of agoraphobia situations

■ Develop lists of superstitious objects, safety signals, distractions, and safety behaviors

Review of Panic Attack and Mood Records

Did you complete a mood record every day and record panic attacks as they occurred over the last week? If not, brainstorm ways of improving your ability to record. Ongoing recording of panic and anxiety is essential to this program. Remember that learning to interrupt your panic and anxiety depends on a complete and accurate description. It is impossible to change without knowing exactly what it is that has to change. In addition, accurate recording becomes more important as you progress through the next few chapters. So, developing good recording habits now will help you complete the rest of the program.

To help you remember to complete the records, place the Daily Mood Record in a visible place, such as on the refrigerator, bathroom mirror, or next to your bed. Also, carry your Panic Attack Records with you wherever you go.

If you have not done any recording, we strongly recommend that you use the following week to record your panic attacks and anxiety before continuing with the program.

If you have kept records over the last week, fill in the data for the first week on the Progress Record: the number of panic attacks for the week, your average daily anxiety rating for the week, and whatever else you decide to chart. Also, look for any patterns from the week's worth of panic attack records. For instance, do the panic attacks typically occur when you are alone or when you are with someone else? Do they occur at a particular time of the day, such as in the evening? Do they occur more often during stressful portions of the day, such as when getting the kids ready for school? Are the symptoms the same each time, or do they vary depending on where the panic occurs? In addition, look for relationships between the Panic Attack Record and the Daily Mood Record. For instance, does panic occur more often when you are feeling generally more anxious or depressed? Does your anxious worry about panic increase after a panic or before a panic?

Looking for patterns moves one closer to understanding that panic is a *reaction* to something. Despite how it feels, panic is not an "out of the blue," automatic response.

Reminder of the Role of Avoidance

It is natural to avoid things that cause anxiety. Anxiety prepares us to avoid things so that we stay out of the way of danger and harm. However, too much anxiety leads to too much avoidance. Although avoidance provides relief from anxiety in the short term, it also causes you to continually feel anxiety in the long term. The longer we avoid the situations that worry or scare us, the scarier or more worrisome they become.

Anxiety ——————▶ Avoidance ——————▶ Anxiety

Avoidance prevents corrective learning (i.e., learning something new). Avoidance behavior is usually connected with overly negative thoughts. For example, if you think you will faint if you drive on the freeway, it makes sense that you would avoid driving on freeways. However, such avoidance prevents you from realizing that your negative thoughts about fainting are wrong. Approaching rather than avoiding situations or experiences is critical to overcoming fear and anxiety. But first, we will identify the specific situations that you avoid and develop skills to help you to approach those situations.

Establishing a Hierarchy of Agoraphobia Situations

Look at the list of agoraphobia situations on page 72. Put a check next to the situations you currently avoid or are anxious about. It may be that there is something you regularly avoid that is not on the list. Put this under "other" at the end. Input as many "others" as is necessary. Now use the situations you have checkmarked to create your own hierarchy of up to 10 items. The list should include mildly anxiety-provoking (i.e., rated at around 3 on a scale of 0 to 10), as well as very anxiety-provoking (i.e., rated at 9 or 10) situations. These will be the situations that you will face over and over again. You may have only one or two situations, or you may have many more than 10 situations that cause you anxiety.

Conditions

Here are some of the conditions to keep in mind which may influence the level of anxiety which you have in each agoraphobia situation. It is very important to include the conditions that make you feel more anxious. For example, if you always feel more anxious when you are alone, it will be essential to include items in your hierarchy in which you are facing situations alone.

Distance From Home

For example, freeway driving may be divided into a number of different tasks, depending on your distance from home (10 minutes from home versus one hour from home). These could be different items on your hierarchy, and it will be important to include further distances from home on your hierarchy if you typically get more anxious the further you are from home.

Proximity to an Exit or Ease of Escape

For example, the task of going to movie theaters may be more or less anxiety provoking, depending on how far into the middle of the row you are seated during the movie. Sitting in the middle of the row may be a lot more anxiety provoking than sitting on the aisle, if it is important to you to be able to get out of wherever you are. Similarly, freeway driving may be easier or more difficult depending on the distances between exit and entrance ramps. If this is the case, make sure that you eventually face situations where exits or escape are very difficult, even though you may start with situations from which there is an easy exit.

Typical Agoraphobia Situations

Check those that apply

Situations You Avoid or Are Anxious About

Driving   _____

Traveling by subway, bus, taxi   _____

Flying   _____

Waiting in lines   _____

Crowds   _____

Stores   _____

Restaurants   _____

Theaters   _____

Long distances from home   _____

Unfamiliar areas   _____

Hairdressers   _____

Long walks   _____

Wide-open spaces   _____

Closed-in spaces (e.g., basements)   _____

Boats   _____

At home alone   _____

Auditoriums   _____

Elevators   _____

Escalators   _____

Other   _____

Time of Day

For example, grocery shopping may be easier or more difficult, depending on whether the shopping is done in the morning, afternoon, or evening. For example, sometimes people are more anxious in the afternoons or evenings because they feel more tired and less able to cope with panic.

Number of People

Whether the situation is crowded or not may influence your level of anxiety. So, shopping during peak hours or driving at peak hours of traffic may be different from shopping or driving when conditions are much less crowded. If this is important to you, include items on your hierarchy that include crowded times.

Accompanied or Alone

Of course, the presence of friends or family often makes a big difference. Relying on certain other people is one form of reliance on a *safety signal* (as described in chapter 1). If you feel less anxious when you have certain people with you, you may begin facing your fear of agoraphobia situations with their aid, but it will be very important for you to eventually face the same situations without those people. So, your hierarchy should include facing situations without the help of others if being alone makes you more anxious.

Summary

In the end, you will practice facing the situations listed on your hierarchy repeatedly, without long intervals between each practice, and in such a way that you derive information that proves your worries to be wrong. Therefore, the conditions have to be the right conditions.

For example, if you worry about fainting only when you are shopping alone and not when you are shopping with a friend or family member, then it will be best to deliberately practice shopping alone. The goal is to provide direct experience that shows that your worries are unrealistic.

So, now list your particular situations, including the conditions that make you most anxious. Then, rate each situation from 0 to 10, where 0 = no anxiety/

Agoraphobia Hierarchy

Situation	Anxiety and/or Avoidance (0–10)
Walk to the store alone (10 blocks)	3
Wait in long line at post office	4
Shop in mall, peak hours	5
Drive to sister's place with family member	6
Drive to sister's place alone	7
Attend live performance at theater	8
Stay overnight in another town	9
Long-distance travel by plane	10

Figure 5.1.

Example of Completed Agoraphobia Hierarchy

do not avoid and 10 = extreme fear/always avoid; ideally, you should have a range of anxiety/avoidance ratings from 3–10. The anxiety/avoidance ratings should be made in terms of how you would feel right now if you were asked to face this particular situation.

If you end up with a lot of items that are below 3 or a lot of items that are above 8, use the list of conditions above to generate a broader distribution of situations. An example of a completed hierarchy is shown here. A blank hierarchy is also provided.

Unhelpful Ways of Coping

Now it is time for you to identify your own unhelpful ways of coping. Eventually, it will be essential to eliminate all of these ways of coping because they are all unhelpful in the long term.

Agoraphobia Hierarchy

Situation	Anxiety and/or Avoidance (0–10)

Superstitious Objects and Safety Signals

As we had already discussed, *superstitious objects* and *safety signals* are objects or people on whom you depend as if they are necessary for your survival. They provide a "sense of safety." Even though they seem to make life easier, in the end, safety signals strengthen fear and avoidance because they reinforce the mistaken idea that panic attacks are harmful. When you understand that there is no real danger, then the need for safety signals is removed. In other words, safety signals do not actually prevent danger because, in reality, there is no danger. However, realizing this comes with experience. In the meantime, it is necessary to know your safety signals.

We have already discussed the roles played by other people. Additional superstitious objects and safety signals include telephones, sunglasses, purses, money (to call for help), paper bags (to breathe into), therapists' phone numbers, relaxation tapes, lucky charms, empty or full medication bottles, antacids, food, and familiar landmarks when travelling. To help you identify your own safety signals, ask yourself what you never leave home without.

Or, to put it another way, consider the things that make you feel more anxious if they are not with you. List these in the space provided on page 77.

This list of superstitious objects and safety signals will be incorporated into your hierarchy in one of two ways. One way is to face each item on your agoraphobia hierarchy first with and then without your safety signals. For example, you might drive two exits on the freeway first with a portable telephone, and then drive the same distance without the telephone. The second way is to eliminate safety signals from the beginning, facing the items on your hierarchy and always doing so without safety signals. The choice between these two approaches is up to you. In fact, for some hierarchy items, you can do it the first way; and for other items on your hierarchy, you can go the second way. Of most importance is that, eventually, you face the agoraphobia situations without your safety signals.

Safety Behaviors and Distractions

Some styles of behaving may reduce anxiety in the short term but are unhelpful in the long term because they interfere with learning mastery. In particular, we are referring to examples of "holding on for dear life," as if the situation that is being faced really is dangerous. Examples include remaining close to structures (such as buildings or rails) to provide a sense of physical support. This is particularly true for persons who fear falling. Remaining close to structures, however, strengthens the mistaken belief that collapsing is likely when "out in the open."

Another example is to keep a tight grip on the steering wheel for fear of losing control. In actuality, it would be quite safe to lessen your grip to a more relaxed level. Other examples of safety behaviors include: placing the parking brake on at traffic lights to keep yourself from losing control of the car and inadvertently driving through a red light; driving very slowly on the freeway; or driving only in the right-hand-side, slow lane and close to exit ramps.

Looking for exits is another safety behavior. For example, you might find yourself searching for exit signs when out at a large nightclub or looking back repeatedly to check on the visibility of the exit sign when shopping inside a mall. Again, the search for an exit is based on the mistaken belief of some danger happening if the situation was inescapable. Exit signs can also function as a safety signal.

Superstitious Objects and Safety Signals

As mentioned earlier, distraction is another band-aid method that contributes to anxiety in the long term. You must eventually face your agoraphobia situations without the aid of distraction. Distraction can be obvious or subtle—but in all cases, it is a way of avoiding the situation. A very common distraction technique is to look away from the object of fear. For example, while you may face heights by ascending to the tenth floor of a building, you may be avoiding them at the same time by refusing to look out of the window or over the edge of the balcony. Similarly, you may face your fear of elevators by using them; but at the same time, you keep your eyes closed during the entire ride.

More subtle methods of distraction include using imagination to pretend to be somewhere else or playing number games or word games until you are out of the tunnel, or after the bridge has been crossed, and so on. Other more dangerous and rare methods of distraction include self-inflicting pain or driving cars at high speeds under the assumption that the fright or pain will overwhelm and wipe out the panic. Of course, in the end, the latter methods of distraction are much more dangerous than a panic attack.

The best results come from an objective focus on one's reactions to a given situation and on the situation itself. Objective self-focus is exemplified by the following type of self-statement: "I'm in the elevator, I can feel it moving, I can see the doors and the ceiling and the floor, I feel my heart beating, and my anxiety is moderate." Objective self-focus differs from subjective self-awareness, which is exemplified by a statement such as: "I feel terrible, I will collapse, I can't make it, I have to get out of here." Subjective focus is probably the style that you naturally engage in since it is part of being anxious and afraid. Most often, attempts to keep distracted alternate with brief but negative moments of subjective self-focus. For example, using counting games or imagery to keep yourself distracted is likely to be interspersed with momentary body-monitoring or questioning how bad you are feeling at a given moment. This combination of distraction and subjective self-focus is likely to contribute to continued anxiety. Your goal is to replace that style with an objective focus that enables you to be fully aware of what is going on.

A goal of this program is to help you eliminate all of your safety behaviors and distractions.

List your typical safety behaviors and distractions in the space provided on page 79.

Safety Behaviors and Distractions

Recognizing your superstitious objects, safety signals, safety behaviors, and distractions is not necessarily an easy task; indeed, we all get into habits of doing things in certain ways without being fully aware of what we are doing. One solution is to ask someone who knows you very well what kinds of things they have observed you do. For example, a husband, wife, sibling, parent, or friend may be aware of subtleties of your behavior of which you are not fully aware.

Homework

✎ Continue to record using your Panic Attack Record and Daily Mood Record.

✎ Read chapter 6, section 1.

Self-Assessment

Answer each of the following by circling T (True) or F (False). Answers are given in the appendix.

1. Avoidance increases anxiety in the short term but decreases anxiety in the long term.   T   F

2. A hierarchy is composed of situations that currently make you anxious and/or that you avoid, with situations ranging from mildly to highly anxious or avoided.   T   F

3. Superstitious objects and safety signals are effective forms of coping with anxiety.   T   F

4. Distracting yourself from anxiety is a sign that you are no longer anxious.   T   F

Chapter 6   *Breathing Skills*

Goals

- To understand how breathing patterns contribute to panic and anxiety

- To learn diaphragmatic breathing

- To learn slow breathing

- To apply breathing skills as a coping skill

We recommend that the information in this chapter be completed over a period of three weeks. Use the table in the introduction to know when to do each section of this chapter in relation to the chapters that follow.

SECTION 1   *Education and Diaphragmatic Breathing*

Am I Breathing Too Much or Not Enough?

Many people *overbreathe* when they panic—in other words, they breathe too quickly. In fact, 50–60% of people who panic show signs of overbreathing. This is also called *hyperventilation.* Technically, to overbreathe or to hyperventilate means to breathe in more oxygen than is needed by the body. Overbreathing is involved in panic attacks in two ways. First, overbreathing may produce an initial physical feeling that frightens you and leads to a panic attack. Second, fear and panic may cause you to overbreathe. The symptoms of overbreathing include dizziness, lightheadedness, shortness of breath, blurred vision, cold sweats, hot flashes and cold chills, feeling faint, a rapid heart rate, tightness or pain around the chest, slurred speech. Although symptoms of overbreathing can be very intense, they are not dangerous.

Let us consider whether overbreathing is an important part of your panics. To do so, answer the following questions.

1. In general, do you often feel short of breath, as if you are not getting enough air?

2. Do you sometimes feel as if you are suffocating?

3. Do you sometimes experience chest pains or pressure around your chest, including symptoms of tingling, prickling, and numbness?

4. Do you yawn or sigh a lot or take in big gulps of air?

5. When you are frightened, do you hold your breath or breathe quickly and shallowly?

If you answered yes to any of those questions, then overbreathing may play at least some part in your panic and anxiety. Of course, if you are like many people, you may not be aware of your breathing patterns. Another way of knowing whether overbreathing is relevant to your panic and anxiety is to conduct the following overbreathing exercise. (*Caution:* Do not do this exercise if you have epilepsy, seizures, or cardiopulmonary diseases.)

Sit in a comfortable chair, and breathe very fast and very deep, as if you are blowing up a balloon. It is important to take the air right down into your lungs and to exhale very forcefully. Continue for as long as you can, for up to two minutes. When you have finished the exercise, close your eyes and breathe slowly, pausing at the end of each breath. Continue the slow breathing for a few minutes, until the physical symptoms have passed.

Now, think about what you experienced. Check off the symptoms from one of your Panic Attack Records. Did you experience symptoms similar to your panic attack symptoms? You may not have been as afraid as is typically the case because you had an obvious explanation for the symptoms (i.e., you deliberately caused the feelings by overbreathing). Nevertheless, were the physical symptoms similar to the symptoms you experience during naturally occurring panic attacks?

If your answer is yes, then overbreathing probably contributes to panic attacks. If not, then overbreathing may not contribute to your panics. Either way, however, learning ways of regulating breathing can be a useful tool for helping you to deal directly with the physical symptoms and situations that you fear and avoid.

Normal Breathing

This brief explanation of the mechanics of breathing and the symptoms of overbreathing will help correct the mistaken belief that the symptoms of overbreathing are harmful.

The body needs oxygen in order to survive. Whenever a person inhales, oxygen is taken into the lungs, where it is picked up by the *hemoglobin* (the "oxygen-sticky" chemical in the blood). The hemoglobin carries the oxygen around the body, where it is released for use by the body's cells. The cells use the oxygen in their energy reactions. After using the oxygen, carbon dioxide is released back into the blood, where it is transported to the lungs and, eventually, exhaled.

The balance between oxygen and carbon dioxide is important, and it is maintained chiefly through an appropriate rate and depth of breathing. Obviously, breathing "too much" will have the effect of increasing levels of oxygen (in the blood only) and decreasing levels of carbon dioxide, while breathing too little will have the effect of decreasing levels of oxygen and increasing levels of carbon dioxide. The appropriate rate of breathing, at rest, is usually around 10–14 breaths per minute.

Hyperventilation is defined as a rate and depth of breathing which is too much for the body's needs at a particular point in time. Naturally, if the need for oxygen and the production of carbon dioxide both increase (such as during exercise), breathing should increase appropriately. Alternately, if the need for oxygen and the production of carbon dioxide both decrease (such as during relaxation), breathing should decrease appropriately.

Anxiety and Overbreathing

Anxiety and fear cause us to increase our breathing because the muscles need more oxygen in order to fight or to flee from danger. If the extra amount of oxygen is not used up at the rate at which it is inhaled (as would be the case if there is no actual running or fighting going on), then the state of hyperventilation, or overbreathing, results.

The most important effect of hyperventilation is to produce a proportionate drop in carbon dioxide (meaning that the amount of carbon dioxide is low in proportion to the amount of oxygen). Our nervous and chemical systems are much more sensitive to levels of carbon dioxide than to levels of oxygen in the blood. A proportionate drop in carbon dioxide in turn produces a drop in the acid content of the blood, leading to what is known as *alkaline blood*. It is these two effects—a proportionate decrease in the blood's level of carbon dioxide and an increase in blood alkalinity—which are responsible for most of the physical changes that occur during hyperventilation.

One of the most important changes produced by hyperventilation is a constriction or narrowing of certain blood vessels around the body. In particular, the blood going to the brain is slightly decreased. Together with this tightening of blood vessels, the hemoglobin increases its "stickiness" for oxygen. Not only does less blood reach certain areas of the body, but also, the oxygen carried by this blood is less likely to be released into the tissues. Although overbreathing means that we are taking in more oxygen than necessary, less oxygen actually gets to certain areas of the brain and body.

This causes two groups of symptoms. First are symptoms produced by the slight reduction in oxygen to certain parts of the brain, including dizziness, lightheadedness, confusion, breathlessness, blurred vision, and feelings of unreality. Second are symptoms produced by the slight reduction in oxygen to certain parts of the body, including an increase in heartbeat (in order to pump more blood around); numbness and tingling in the extremities; cold, clammy hands; and, sometimes, stiffness of the muscles. It is important to remember that the reductions in oxygen are slight and totally harmless. Also, hyperventilating can produce a feeling of breathlessness, sometimes extending to feelings of choking or smothering, so that it actually feels as if there is not enough air.

Hyperventilation also causes other effects. First, the act of overbreathing is hard physical work. It can make you feel hot, flushed, and sweaty, and after prolonged periods, it will often cause tiredness and exhaustion. Also, people who overbreathe often breathe from their chest rather than their diaphragm (the muscle beneath the rib cage). When chest muscles are used predominantly, they become tired and tender from overuse. This sometimes causes chest tightness or even severe chest pains. Finally, many people who overbreathe have a habit of sighing or yawning. Unfortunately, these contribute to the problem because yawning and sighing cause large quantities of carbon dioxide to be dumped out of the system very quickly, lowering the proportionate amount of carbon dioxide in the blood.

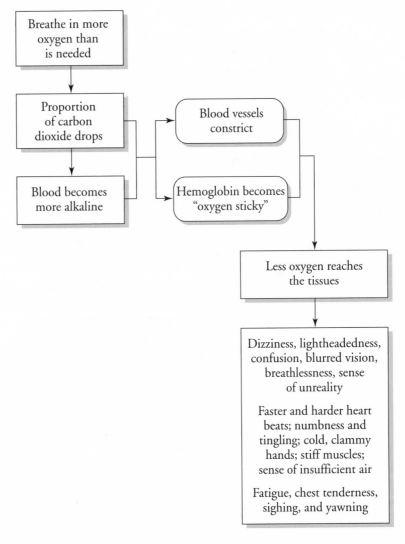

Figure 6.1.

Physical Changes Caused by Overbreathing

Hyperventilation is not always obvious, especially with mild overbreathing for a long period of time. In this case, there can be a large proportionate drop in carbon dioxide. Due to compensation in the body, the blood-acidity level returns to normal. Thus, symptoms are not present all of the time. However, because carbon dioxide levels remain low, the body loses its ability to cope with changes in breathing. Even a slight change in breathing (e.g., through a yawn or by climbing a set of stairs) can be enough to suddenly cause the symptoms to appear. This may explain the sudden nature of many panic attacks—a small change in breathing in someone who has a general tendency to overbreathe, even if only mildly, causes acute hyperventilation.

Probably the most important point to be made about hyperventilation is that it is not dangerous.

Breathing Skills: Diaphragm Breathing

Next is a specific exercise to teach the skill of diaphragmatic breathing. The purpose of this exercise is to learn a method of regulating breathing that will help you to deal directly with the physical symptoms and situations that currently make you anxious. This breathing skill is not designed to control or prevent feelings of fear and anxiety; rather, it is intended to help you face feelings of fear and anxiety and the situations in which they arise.

The exercise involves a breathing component, in which you learn to slow your breathing and to breathe using your diaphragm muscle more than the chest muscles, and a meditation component. Meditation means to focus your attention on the exercise of breathing. As with all skills, learning to meditate requires practice.

The following exercise should be practiced at least twice a day, for at least 10 minutes each time. At first, the exercise may be hard, but it will get easier the more that you do it.

Step One

The first step is to concentrate on taking breaths right down to your stomach (or, more accurately, to your diaphragm muscles).

- There should be an expansion (increase) of the stomach every time you breathe in, or inhale. The stomach is sucked back in every time you breathe out, or exhale.

- If you are having trouble taking the air down to your stomach, place one hand on your chest and the other hand on your stomach with the little finger about one inch above the belly button. As you breathe in and out, only the hand on your stomach should move. If you are correctly doing the exercise, there should not be much movement from the hand on your chest. If you are normally a chest breather, this may feel artificial and cause feelings of breathlessness. That is a natural response—just remember that you are getting enough oxygen and that the feelings of breathlessness will decrease the more that you practice.

Step Two

The second step is to breathe in normal amounts of air. Do not take in too much air, as it should not be a big breath.

- At this stage, breathe at your normal rate—do not try to slow down your breathing. We will work on slowing your breathing later.

- Also, keep your breathing smooth. Do not gulp in a big breath and then let it out all at once. When you breathe out, think of the air as oozing and escaping from your nose or mouth rather than being suddenly blown out. It does not matter whether you breathe through your nose or your mouth, as long as you breathe smoothly.

Step Three

The third step involves meditation. You will count every time that you breathe in and think the word "relax" as you breathe out.

- That is, when you breathe in, think "one" to yourself; and as you breathe out, think the word "relax." Think "two" on your next breath in, and think "relax" on the breath out. Think "three" on your next breath in, and think "relax" on the breath out. Continue this until you count to around "10," and then go back to "one."

- Focus only on your breathing and the words. This can be very difficult, and you may never be able to do it perfectly. You may not get past the first number without other thoughts coming into your mind. This is natural. When this happens, do not get angry or give up. Simply allow the thoughts to pass through your mind, and then bring your attention back to the breathing, the numbers, and the words.

Practice twice a day (or more, if you want to), about 10 minutes each time, in relaxing situations, such as a quiet place at home where you will not be disturbed.

This new way of breathing may feel strange at first and cause feelings of breathlessness. That is natural. Just remember that you are getting enough air and that it will get easier the more you practice.

For now, do not use this new type of calm breathing at times of anxiety because trying to use a strategy that is only partially developed can be more frustrating and anxiety producing than not trying it at all. It would be like teaching scuba divers a way of dealing with underwater emergencies one time and then expecting them to use the skill successfully in an actual underwater emergency. Instead, scuba divers must practice the emergency procedure on land over and over again before using it underwater. So, for now, the breathing exercises should only be done in a quiet, comfortable environment. Once you have become skilled in the basic exercise of calm breathing, then we will apply it as a coping skill for anxiety.

After each practice, record your levels of concentration on the breathing and counting and the success with which you are able to use your diaphragm muscle by using the Breathing Skills Record. You may photocopy this form from the book or download multiple copies at the Treatments *ThatWork*™ website (http://www.oup.com/us/ttw). Each form should last one week. This will provide feedback for you and your doctor or mental health professional.

Remember that even if you cannot successfully learn this breathing skill, you are not in danger. This skill is helpful for the regulation of breathing, but it is not necessary.

Homework

✎ Continue recording your panic attacks and your daily mood using the Panic Attack Record and the Daily Mood Record. At the end of each week, add the number of panic attacks and your daily average anxiety to your Progress Record.

Breathing Skills Record

Rate your concentration on breathing and counting during the exercise and your success with relying mostly on your diaphragm for breathing, on 0–10-point scales (where 0 = none and 10 = excellent), after each practice (twice per day).

0 ------- 1 ------- 2 ------- 3 ------- 4 ------- 5 ------- 6 ------- 7 ------- 8 ------- 9 ------- 10

None   Mild   Moderate   Strong   Excellent

Date	Practice	Concentration on Breathing and Counting	Success With Breathing
	1		
	2		
	1		
	2		
	1		
	2		
	1		
	2		
	1		
	2		
	1		
	2		
	1		
	2		
	1		
	2		
	1		
	2		

✎ Practice the diaphragm-breathing exercise twice a day, for 10 minutes each time, for seven days. Keep a record of your practices on the Breathing Skills Record.

Continue with section 2 of this chapter after you have completed one week of practicing diaphragm breathing.

Self-Assessment

Answer each of the following by circling T (True) or F (False). Answers are given in the appendix.

1. *Overbreathing* means breathing too much and too deeply for the body's needs at a particular point in time. T F

2. Continuous overbreathing is potentially dangerous. T F

3. When practicing breathing skills exercises, one should focus on completely unrelated material. T F

4. Feelings of dizziness and discomfort as you practice diaphragmatic breathing are an indication that you should discontinue the breathing exercises. T F

5. The goals of breathing skills are to eliminate fear and anxiety. T F

6. The goals of breathing skills are to help you deal directly with the physical symptoms and situations that make you anxious. T F

SECTION 2   *Review and Slowed Breathing*

Review of Breathing Skills Practice

Did you feel as if you were getting the air down toward your abdomen, as you would if you were mostly using your diaphragm muscle? Are you getting symptoms of anxiety when you practice? If so, this is probably due to breathing a little fast or becoming anxious about your breathing as you pay attention to it. Keep practicing, and the anxiety will diminish. Are you having trouble concentrating on the counting? Practice will help your concentration. Simply redirect your attention back to the breath and the words (i.e., the numbers and the word "relax") each time you notice your mind wandering.

Breathing Skills: Slowed Breathing

This exercise is designed to slow your breathing rate by matching your breathing to your counting. Practice two times per day, for 10 minutes each time, for seven days, in a comfortable, quiet location.

- Count the number, and *then* inhale; think the word "relax," and *then* exhale. In other words, put a little pause between each time you inhale and each time you exhale.

- Breathe at a rate of around 10 breaths per minute. This means to count (one second), inhale (two seconds), think the word "relax" (one second), and then exhale (two seconds). Every breath will take a total of six seconds from when you count to when you finish exhaling, which means 10 total breaths per minute. This does not have to be perfectly timed, but aim for something close to 10 breaths per minute.

- You may continue to practice with one hand on your stomach and one hand on your chest in order to encourage deep (i.e., diaphragm) breathing.

- The main goals are to slow down your breathing while maintaining a smooth and fluid flow of air and to use the diaphragm more than the chest.

- Remember to think of the air as oozing and escaping from your nose or mouth rather than being suddenly blown out, and remember to take a normal-size breath rather than a big breath.

Homework

✎ Continue recording your panic attacks and daily mood using the Panic Attack Record and the Daily Mood Record. At the end of each week, add the number of panic attacks and average daily anxiety to your Progress Record.

✎ Practice the slowed breathing exercise twice a day, 10 minutes each time, for seven days. Keep a record of your practices on the Breathing Skills Record.

✎ Continue with section 3 of this chapter after you have completed one week of slowed breathing practice.

Self-Assessment

Answer each of the following by circling T (True) or F (False). Answers are given in the appendix.

1. Skipping out on practices of breathing skills every now and then is okay.   T   F

2. To slow my breathing means to count to 10 as I breathe in and to count to 10 as I breathe out.   T   F

3. If it is not any easier by now, then breathing skills training is never going to work.   T   F

4. Breathing skills are not designed to eliminate physical symptoms of anxiety or panic.   T   F

Breathing Skills

Now that you are able to breathe at a slower rate, it is time to practice in different places, not just in relaxing places. Do the breathing exercise when you are at work, watching television, or out socially. Do as many mini-practices as you can during the day. That is, instead of a full 10 minutes, practice for a minute or two wherever you are, sitting at a traffic light, listening to someone else talk to you over the telephone, or while you are in the shower.

Also, now it is time to apply breathing skills as a technique for helping you to face anxiety and situations that bother you. In other words, as you feel anxious symptoms building, begin to concentrate on slow, smooth diaphragmatic breathing. Count on your inhalations, and think the word "relax" on the exhalations. Continue by counting 1–10 and then 10 back down to 1, slowing the breathing rate to about three seconds on the inhalation and three seconds on the exhalation. Remember, the goal is not to eliminate anxiety but rather to regulate your breathing, interrupt the panic cycle, and help you to go ahead and face the things that are making you feel anxious. Breathing skills are intended to move you forward, so that you can face and overcome your fears rather than hide from them. Use the breathing skills to help you "breath through" fear and anxiety.

Also, remember that even if you do not control the symptoms of breathlessness, you are not in danger. This is very important. To believe that you must slow your breathing to prevent yourself from losing control, having a heart attack, or experiencing some other catastrophe adds unnecessary anxiety to the breathing exercise. Remember, hyperventilation is not dangerous.

You may discontinue the two daily, 10-minute practices of breathing skills at this point, especially if you are easily able to breathe slowly from your diaphragm muscle. However, it does not hurt to continue the two daily practices, alongside the frequent mini-practices, especially if it remains difficult at times to achieve slow and diaphragmatic breathing.

Homework

✎ Continue recording your panic attacks and daily mood using the Panic Attack Record and Daily Mood Record. At the end of the week, add the number of panic attacks and daily average anxiety to your Progress Record.

✎ Practice breathing skills in different, distracting environments, whenever possible.

✎ Apply breathing skills to help you continue in whatever activity or situation makes you anxious.

✎ Continue with section 4 after you have completed one week of practicing breathing skills in different environments and with moments of anxiety.

Self-Assessment

Answer each of the following by circling T (True) or F (False). Answers are given in the appendix.

1. Practicing breathing skills in different environments is designed to prevent any anxiety or panic.　　　　T　　F

2. When I become anxious, it is important to leave the situation that I am currently facing and practice slow breathing, so that I can calm myself down and then go home.　　　　T　　F

3. Breathing skills are intended to help me face situations and things that make me anxious.　　　　T　　F

Review of Breathing Through Anxiety and Panic

Did you use your breathing skills when you felt anxious as a way of helping you to continue whatever you were doing? What was the effect? Were you able to pick up on early signals of physical discomfort, or was it not until you found yourself gasping for breath that you tried the breathing exercise? If this was the case, become more aware of early signs that can prompt you to engage the breathing skills. Did you try the breathing exercise with a sense of desperation, to escape or prevent at all costs the symptoms of anxiety? If so, remember that the purpose of the breathing skills is not to prevent fear and anxiety but rather to enable you to do whatever you have to do, and continue moving forward, even though you may be anxious or panicky. If you are using breathing control with desperation (e.g., "If I don't slow down my breathing, I may die"), you will only add fuel to the fire and, therefore, increase your panic and anxiety. Remember, even if you never learn to slow your breathing or to breath from your diaphragm muscles, you will survive. The goal is to use the breathing skills to help you face whatever is making you anxious; eventually, the anxiety will decrease.

Homework

✎ Continue recording your panic attacks and daily mood using the Panic Attack Record and Daily Mood Record. At the end of the week, add the number of panic attacks and daily average anxiety to your Progress Record.

✎ Continue to practice breathing skills in different, distracting environments, whenever possible.

✎ Continue to apply breathing skills to help you continue in whatever activity or situation makes you anxious.

Chapter 7 — *Thinking Skills*

Goals

- To understand how thoughts influence our emotions

- To discover your negative thoughts

- To understand errors of jumping to conclusions and seeing things out of perspective

- To learn how to develop realistic odds

- To learn how to put things into perspective

We recommend that the information in this chapter be completed over a period of three weeks. Use the table in the introduction to know when to do each section of this chapter in relation to the chapters to follow.

In earlier chapters, we discussed the importance of thoughts and, in particular, how negative thoughts can contribute to the snowballing cycles of anxiety and panic. In this chapter, you will build skills for changing your mistaken beliefs and negative thoughts.

SECTION 1 — *Thoughts Influence Emotions*

Imagine a friend walking toward you. Instead of smiling and saying "Hello," this person walks straight past you without even acknowledging you. What might you think about this? If you think that the person is angry or upset with you, then you might feel anxious or depressed. If you think that the person is stressed out by something else and did not even notice you, then you might feel very little emotion or, perhaps, even feel compassion for them. Of course, this is relevant to panic disorder in that the ways in which you think about physical symptoms will influence how you feel about physical symptoms. Below is an example of different ways of thinking about the physical symptom of pain in your chest and about the emotional

Table 7.1. Examples of the Influence of Thoughts About Physical Symptoms on Emotions

Event	+	Thoughts About the Event	=	Emotion
Pain in chest		Sign of heart attack		Panic
Pain in chest		Sign of indigestion		No panic
Pain in chest		Sign of muscle strain		No panic
Pain in chest		Sign of cancer		Panic
Pain in chest		Sign of tension and stress		No panic

effect, which is similar to the panic cycle that we described in chapters 3 and 4.

The same is true for different ways of thinking about agoraphobia situations, as shown below.

Emotions Influence Thoughts

In addition, negative emotions cause more negative thoughts: feeling afraid increases the likelihood of having negative thoughts. This is because the number-one effect of the fight-flight system is to alert us to the possibility

Table 7.2. Examples of the Influence of Thoughts About Agoraphobia Situations on Emotions

Event	+	Thoughts About the Event	=	Emotion
Elevator is old and slow		Elevator will get stuck; I will be trapped, panic, and make fool of myself		Panic/Anxiety
Elevator is old and slow		Elevator is unlikely to get stuck; and even if it does get stuck, I will be able to handle it		No Panic/ Anxiety
Stomach cramps during a meeting		Embarrassed to leave; will not get to bathroom in time		Panic/Anxiety
Stomach cramps during meeting		No big deal if I leave; I can always make it to bathroom		No panic/ Anxiety

Table 7.3. Examples of the Influence of Emotions on Thoughts

Emotion	+	Event	=	Thoughts About the Event
Already anxious about walking away from home		Pain in chest		More likely to think of heart attack, cannot make it home
Relaxed about walking away from home		Pain in chest		More likely to think of indigestion or muscle strain

of danger. However, sometimes an obvious threat cannot be found. It is very difficult for us to accept not having an explanation for feelings of panic. (We talked about this in chapters 3 and 4.) When people cannot find an obvious explanation for their feelings, they turn their search on themselves. In other words, "If nothing out there is making me feel afraid, then there must be something wrong with me." In this case, the brain invents an explanation, such as "I must be dying, losing control, or going insane." As you can see from the information provided in chapters 3 and 4, nothing could be farther from the truth. The purpose of the fight-flight system is to protect the organism, not to harm it—it is our survival mechanism.

The effect of being anxious on the ways in which we think is shown above.

The fact that anxiety produces more negative thoughts helps explain why, when feeling calm, many recognize that their panic attacks will not cause them harm; but when in the midst of panic, the same people are convinced that their panic attacks are harmful.

Emotions and Thoughts Cycle

So, panic and anxiety produce negative thoughts, and negative thoughts produce panic and anxiety. In the end, a cycle of negative thoughts and panic and anxiety develops. For all these reasons, learning to change the thoughts that contribute to anxiety and panic is very important.

At this point, you might think, "I don't tell myself anything when I panic, it just comes out of the blue." There is a dimension of awareness to our thinking. That is, sometimes we are fully aware of our thoughts; and at other times, our thoughts are so automatic that we do not even know what we are thinking. As an example of the latter, think of driving a car. There are many, many thoughts that go on as you pull out from a parking place (e.g., put my foot on the accelerator, put my foot on the brake, turn the wheel this way, look over my shoulder, pull out slowly, and so on). However, you probably are not aware of those thoughts. Thoughts are more likely to become automatic the more often we think them. So, for example, if you have believed for a long time that panic attacks cause heart disease, then that thought may occur without you being aware that that is what you are thinking—the thinking becomes automatic. Nevertheless, by careful self-observation, we can usually dig up our automatic thoughts.

Go to each item on your Hierarchy of Agoraphobia Situations and to each panic attack that you have recorded over the last week. For each agoraphobia situation, ask yourself, "What will happen if I am forced to enter and remain in that situation?" For each panic attack, ask yourself, "What did I think could happen?"

Now it is time to be as detailed as you can. That is, rather than saying, "I thought I could panic," list the different negative possibilities that came across your mind, even if only for a brief second, such as "If I panic, I might die from a heart attack." If your descriptions of your thoughts are general, such as "I felt horrible" or "I will feel anxious," ask yourself: "Why was it so terrible? What did I think could happen?" Or, if your thought was "I could lose control," ask yourself what could have happened if you did lose control. In other words, be more specific than simply stating that you are afraid of panicking or afraid of becoming anxious in a situation. Panic and anxiety are emotional states in the same way that anger and excitement and sadness are emotional states. They are not inherently dangerous. When you say that you are afraid of having a panic attack, then it means that the panic signifies something bad happening to you, such as physical injury (heart attack, stroke, fainting), going insane, losing control, dying, or being shunned and embarrassed. These are the negative thoughts—the catastrophes—that contribute to the panic cycle.

Similarly, if your initial thought is that you are afraid of being trapped or that it will be too difficult to get out of a situation, think more about the reasons why that worries you. Remember, the need to escape from a situation is only relevant to the degree that you think something bad will happen if you are forced to stay in the situation. It may help to think of yourself as being literally trapped in your feared situation (e.g., imagine yourself stuck in an elevator or on a very long plane trip), and ask yourself what motivates you to want to leave. For example, the fear of being trapped might be based on fears of shouting, screaming, and hurting people in order to get out.

Here is an example from a discussion between a therapist and a client with panic disorder. The therapist is helping the client to identify the negative thoughts in as much detail as possible.

T: *What do you mean when you say that the feeling of a racing heart is horrible? What is horrible about it?*

C: *Well—it makes me feel very scared.*

T: *What are you scared of?*

C: *It makes me worry about something going wrong—physically.*

T: *What do you think could happen?*

C: *Maybe my heart will just keep going faster and faster, and eventually, it will stop.*

T: *And then what?*

C: *Well, then I'll die.*

T: *What about your fears of totally losing control? What do you mean by that?*

C: *That's hard to describe. I guess I don't really know what it means. I just feel out of control.*

T: *What do you think could happen if you were totally out of control?*

C: *That I couldn't stop the way I was feeling.*

T: *And what would happen if you couldn't stop that feeling?*

C: *Well, the feeling would get so intense that I wouldn't be able to function anymore. I'd just be a wreck.*

T: *And then what?*

C: *That would be the end of my life. I'd spend the rest of my life doing nothing.*

Use this type of approach to discover your thoughts for each panic attack over the past week and for each item on your Hierarchy of Agoraphobia Situations. List the details on the Negative Thoughts form provided on page 103. Remember, the method is to ask yourself, "What am I afraid of?" and to follow up with questions such as, "And if that were to happen, then what?" or "And if that were to happen, what would that mean?" With this amount of detail, it is easier to eventually dispel mistaken beliefs. So, continue questioning yourself until you find the specific negative predictions that you are making.

Once you have identified the details of your thoughts in each agoraphobia situation and in each panic attack, continue with Section 2.

SECTION 2   *Jumping to Conclusions and Realistic Odds*

Mistakes in Anxious Thinking

Years of research have shown that when we become anxious or panicky, we make two mistakes in our thinking. The mistakes are: (1) to jump to conclusions about negative events and (2) to blow things out of proportion. These mistakes lead us to believe that events are more dangerous than they really are and to make us more anxious. It is important to learn how to correct those mistakes.

Jumping to Conclusions About Negative Events

To jump to conclusions means to believe an event to be much more likely to happen than it really is. Can you think of times when you caught yourself jumping to a negative conclusion only to find out later that you were

Negative Thoughts

1. _____

_____

2. _____

_____

3. _____

_____

4. _____

_____

5. _____

_____

6. _____

_____

7. _____

_____

8. _____

_____

9. _____

_____

10. _____

_____

wrong? Maybe you were sure that you would not get tickets into the theater because you were at the end of the line, and then you did. Maybe you were convinced that someone was going to be upset with you, and they were not. This means that you were inflating the likelihood of a negative event. Now think about your panic and anxiety. How many times have you thought that something terribly wrong would happen, and how many times has it actually happened? Most often, you will find that what you are afraid of has never happened or has happened only rarely. For example, how many times have you thought that you might faint, and how many times have you actually fainted? Or, how many times have you thought that you would lose control and start screaming, and how many times has that actually happened? The fact that these things do not happen shows you that you are jumping to conclusions.

You might say, "Yes, I know those things are probably not going to happen, but I still get frightened by the possibility." Why do these mistaken beliefs persist? There are several reasons why you might believe that bad events could still happen in future panic attacks.

Perhaps you have consistently avoided what you are really afraid of, so that you have not gathered evidence to the contrary. For example, perhaps you have avoided driving on freeways because of the mistaken belief that you might lose control of the car or pass out at the wheel. However, by avoiding driving, you have not given yourself the opportunity to learn that those things—losing control of the car or passing out—do not happen very often. This is one of the reasons why it is so important to face your fears.

Maybe you think that what has happened in past panic attacks is not good evidence for what could happen in future panic attacks. However, for the most part, past experience is a good predictor of future experience. For example, if you have never fainted up until now, then chances are that you will not faint in the future. This is because the chances of fainting (or whatever else it is that you are afraid of) are pretty much the same each time that you panic.

Or, maybe you think that the only reason why you have survived previous panic attacks is because of luck or because of something that you or someone else did at the time. This kind of reasoning leads to the belief that catastrophes could still happen in the future. For example, some people think that the only reason why they did not faint was because they managed to sit down just in time or to get help just in time. In actuality, they would not have fainted even if they had remained standing or if they had not gotten help. Other examples are: "I only made it because I managed to get to the hospital in time"; "If my wife hadn't been there to help me, I could have died"; "I would have had a heart attack if I hadn't lain down and rested." Taking the last example: in reality, the heart attack did not occur because the real chances of heart attack at that moment of panic are very, very small, regardless of how intense the symptoms are, regardless of whether you are in a hospital emergency room or at home, regardless of whether you are alone or accompanied, and regardless of whether you are lying down or remaining active.

Sometimes, people think that catastrophes have indeed happened to them when, in reality, they have not. For example, sometimes the feeling of panic and the urge to escape are seen as evidence for actual loss of control. (We discussed this before, when describing common myths about panic symptoms.) In reality, actions are guided by whatever is regarded as the safest thing to do at that moment, given whatever it is that is feared could happen. For example, if you believe that you are about to stop breathing, then it makes sense to run outside into fresh air. If you believe that you are about to have a stroke, then it makes sense to go to a hospital. If you believe that you are losing touch with reality forever, it makes sense to pinch yourself or even to pinch someone else to get back that feeling of reality. The mistake is to think that these types of behaviors show that you are out of control; in fact, what they do show is that you have mistaken beliefs about panic attacks.

Another reason is the mistaken belief that the stronger the anxiety or bodily symptoms, the more likely it is that the catastrophe will happen. For example, "I know I haven't lost all touch with reality yet, but what if the feelings get worse than ever before? Then I really could flip out." Or, "If my heart races any faster, then it will explode." In reality, the intensity of the physical symptoms is not evidence for them being more harmful. A similar belief is that the chances of harm increase over time because the damaging effects of each panic attack add on to each other. For example, some people believe that their heart is damaged with each panic attack and, therefore, that their heart will eventually give way if the panic attacks continue. As described in the previous section, there is no evidence that the body or nervous system is worn down in this way. General stress and worry may eventually have an effect on your body, but panic attacks themselves do not have this kind of negative effect over time.

A final reason why beliefs in catastrophes persist is because of something that we mentioned before—that negative thoughts become automatic, like a habit. That is, negative thoughts will come into your mind when you are anxious just through habit and despite the fact that your thinking is more logical at other times.

Some of these types of reasoning are illustrated below in the interaction between Jane and her therapist.

> JANE: *I thought I was really going to lose it this time, that I would flip out and never return to reality. It never actually happened, but it could still happen.*
>
> THERAPIST: *What makes you think that it could still happen?*
>
> JANE: *Part of me feels like I've always managed to escape it just in time, by either removing myself from the situation, or by having my husband help me, or by holding on long enough for the feelings to pass. But what if, next time, I can't hold on?*
>
> THERAPIST: *Have you ever flipped out and lost touch with reality?*
>
> JANE: *I suppose you're saying that, in reality, I can always hold on or that I can always escape in time.*
>
> THERAPIST: *Not really, but rather, that you are jumping to a conclusion that if you do not hold on or do not escape, then you will flip out and never return to reality.*
>
> JANE: *But it really feels like I will.*
>
> THERAPIST: *The confusion between what you think will happen and what actually happens is the very problem that we are addressing in this phase of the treatment.*

Examine the Evidence and Develop Realistic Odds

Treat Thoughts as Guesses

As we discussed before, fear and anxiety lead us to have mistaken beliefs; and, in turn, those mistaken beliefs contribute to fear and anxiety. In other words, jumping to conclusions about negative events and blowing things out of proportion make us feel anxious and afraid. The first step toward change is to treat thoughts as guesses rather than as facts. Once you recognize them as being guesses instead of facts, then you are in a position to recognize that your thoughts may be mistaken and, therefore, that they should be tested by looking at the evidence. Are your beliefs supported by evidence or not? The goal is to develop more realistic ways of thinking. This is not the same as positive thinking. In the long run, the "Don't worry, be happy" notion, where we pretend that everything is okay, is not very helpful. But it does help to say, "Wait a minute, maybe I am thinking about this in the wrong way—maybe the chances of me dying the next time I panic are small." Or: "Even if others did notice that I looked anxious, maybe it wouldn't be as bad as I thought."

Evidence-Based Thinking

More realistic beliefs can be developed by considering all of the evidence—and from obtaining additional information, where necessary—such as the information covered earlier in this workbook. To consider the evidence, ask yourself, "What are the real odds of this happening, has this ever happened before, what is the evidence that it will or will not happen?" This means that you must look at all of the facts before you judge how likely something is. Examining the evidence helps us to see that negative events are less likely to happen than we first thought.

For example, you may assume that you will fail a test; but in so doing, you have ignored the fact that you have prepared carefully. Or, a friend may be acting coldly, and you may think that they are displeased with you but overlook the possibility that they are angry at someone else or that they have had a bad day. In terms of panic attacks, you may think that tingling in the left arm is a sign of a heart attack and thus overlook the fact that you are in good health and that you have experienced the tingling many times before without having had a heart attack. Or, you may worry about panicking at the meeting and overlook the fact that, despite occasional panics in meetings, there have been many times when you did not panic in meetings. Similarly, you may think that you are going to faint while overlooking the fact that you have never fainted before and that people rarely faint during panic attacks. Or, you may think that you will lose control and scream wildly while ignoring the fact that you have never done that before. Also, you may think that the panic will reach such an intense level that it never ends or cause you permanent damage while ignoring the fact that this has never happened before and ignoring the data about our inbuilt mechanisms, which restore balance (i.e., the parasympathetic nervous system) so that panics never continue forever. Or, you may think that the sense of disorientation you are experiencing means that you will go insane like the other person you knew who also was disoriented and who had become mentally ill; but you are overlooking the fact that there are many, many differences between you and the other person.

Then, after considering the evidence, rate the actual odds of the event that you are worried about. Rate the odds on a 0–100 point scale, where 0 = It will never happen and 100 = It will definitely happen. This rating is based on the evidence and not on how you feel. So, look at all of the data and evidence. The probabilities are very helpful for developing more realistic ways of thinking. Odds are more objective than a statement of "I think it could happen" or "I think it probably will not happen."

After you have recorded the realistic odds, generate alternative thoughts that are based on the data and evidence to replace the negative thought. All the different thoughts can be viewed as pieces of a pie. The example pro-

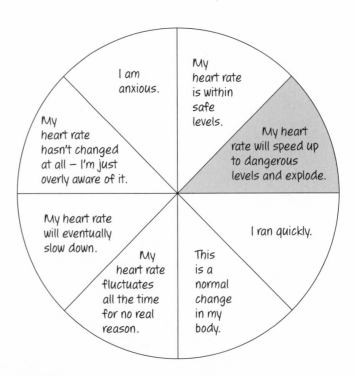

Figure 7.1.

Example of Completed Realistic Odds Pie Chart

vided below shows different ways of thinking about an increase in heart rate. The negative thought is shaded. The greater number of alternative thoughts in comparison to your one negative thought indicates the low likelihood of your negative thought actually coming to pass.

The importance of looking at the evidence for the negative event is seen in the following interchange between Jane and her therapist.

THERAPIST: *One of your negative thoughts is that you will flip out and never return to reality [negative event]. What leads you to think that this is likely to happen?*

JANE: *Well, I guess it really feels like that.*

THERAPIST: *Be more specific, if you can. What feelings?*

JANE: *Well, I feel spacey and unreal, like things around me are different and that I'm not connected [reasoning for negative event].*

THERAPIST: *And why do you think those feelings mean that you have lost touch with reality?*

JANE: *I don't know—it just feels as if I have.*

THERAPIST: *I see—let's look at some of the evidence. Do you respond if someone asks you a question at those times?*

JANE: *Well, I respond to you even though I feel that way sometimes in here.*

THERAPIST: *Okay, and can you walk or write or drive when you feel that way?*

JANE: *Yes, but it feels different.*

THERAPIST: *So, it sounds like you perform those functions despite feeling detached. What does that tell you?*

JANE: *Well, maybe I haven't lost complete touch with reality. But what if I do?*

THERAPIST: *How many times have you felt detached?*

JANE: *Hundreds of times.*

THERAPIST: *And how many times have you lost touch with reality permanently?*

JANE: *Never. But what if the feelings don't go away? Maybe I'll lose it then.*

THERAPIST: *So what else tells you that this is a possibility?*

JANE: *What about my second cousin? He lost it when he was about 25, and now, he's just a mess. He can hardly do anything on his own, and he is constantly in and out of psychiatric wards. They have him on a bunch of heavy-duty medications. I'll never forget the time I saw him totally out of it—he was talking to himself in gibberish.*

THERAPIST: *So, you think you'll be like your cousin. Are there things that are different between you and him? It sounds like he may have something like schizophrenia.*

JANE: *Yes, that is what I was told.*

THERAPIST: *So, let's consider all of the evidence and some alternatives. You have felt unreal hundreds of times, and you've never lost touch with reality because you've continued to function in the midst of those feelings, and they have never lasted forever. You are afraid of becoming like your cousin, but he is suffering from schizophrenia, and your panic attacks are completely different from schizophrenia. Also, keep in mind our previous discussion of where feelings of unreality can come from—from being physically tense and from overbreathing. So, what are the realistic odds that you will lose touch with reality permanently? Use a 0–100 point scale, where 0 = No chance at all and 100 = Definitely will happen.*

JANE: *Well, maybe it is lower than I thought. Maybe 20%.*

THERAPIST: *So, that would mean that you have actually lost touch with reality in a permanent way once every five times you have felt unreal?*

JANE: *When it's put like that, I guess not. Maybe it's a very small possibility.*

THERAPIST: *Yes, so what is a different way of thinking about the feelings of unreality?*

JANE: *Perhaps feeling anxious or overbreathing causes them, and they don't mean that I am losing touch with reality or that I am like my cousin.*

Changing Your Own Odds

Look at your list of Negative Thoughts, and identify examples of where you were jumping to conclusions. (i.e. concerns about a negative event that you frequently worry over but that has never happened or has only rarely occurred.) Then, examine the evidence for each example by completing the following steps, using the Changing Your Odds form as you go. You may photocopy this form from the book or download multiple copies at the Treatments *ThatWork*™ website (http://www.oup.com/us/ttw).

I. Has what I am worried about ever come true?

II. What are the mistaken reasons why I continue to worry?
- Have I avoided the situations that would help me gain a more realistic understanding?
- Am I mistakenly thinking that evidence from past panic attacks does not apply to future panic attacks?
- Am I mistakenly thinking that I have been lucky or that things that I have done in the moment of panic have actually saved me from negative things happening?
- Am I mistakenly thinking that the negative thing I worry about has actually already come true, when in fact, it has not?
- Am I mistakenly thinking that the risk of negative things happening increases with the intensity of panic and anxiety?

III. What is the evidence?
- Ask yourself the following.
  a. "What is the evidence to suggest that it will happen?"
  b. "What is the evidence to suggest that it will not happen?"
- Remember to not confuse your behaviors with the evidence regarding what you are most worried about. For example, if you believe that you are about to stop breathing, then it makes sense to run outside into fresh air. However, it is incorrect to view these

behaviors as signs of a loss of control; they are logical actions, given the anxious thoughts.

■ Consider whether you are confusing low probabilities (odds) with high probabilities (odds) or acting and feeling as if negative results are guaranteed to occur, as opposed to being just possible.

IV. What are the actual odds?

■ Rate the actual odds of whatever it is that you are most worried about after having considered all of the evidence.

■ Rate the odds on a 0–100 point scale, where 0 = It will never happen and 100 = It will definitely happen.

0 ----- 10 ----- 20 ----- 30 ----- 40 ----- 50 ----- 60 ----- 70 ----- 80 ----- 90 ----- 100

| Never will happen | Slight chance | Moderate chance | Strong chance | Definitely will happen |

V. What are different ways of thinking that are more based in evidence?

■ Use a pie chart to list different ways of thinking.

■ Think of as many different ways of thinking as you can along-side your negative thoughts as one piece (the shaded piece) of the pie chart.

Homework

✎ Continue recording your panic attacks and daily mood using the Panic Attack Record and Daily Mood Records. At the end of the week, add the number of your panic attacks and your average daily anxiety to your Progress Record.

✎ Practice Changing Your Odds for each example of jumping to conclusions from your list of Negative Thoughts, as well as for any panic attacks that occur over this next week.

✎ After one week, continue on to section 3 of this chapter.

Changing Your Odds

Negative thought: _____

_____

How many times has it happened? _____

Reasons why I continue to worry about it: _____

   1. Avoidance behavior _____

   2. Mistaken belief that past evidence does not apply _____

   3. Mistaken belief that luck or my extra-cautious behaviors have prevented it from happening _____

   4. Mistaken belief that what I most worried about has come true _____

   5. Mistaken belief that dangers increase with intensity of anxiety or physical symptoms _____

What is the evidence? _____

_____

_____

_____

What are the real odds? (0–100) _____

What are different thoughts? *(Fill in the pie chart, including your anxious thoughts as the shaded piece of the pie):*

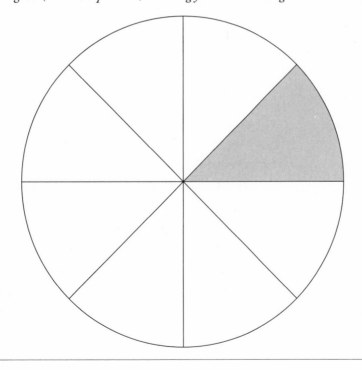

Answer each of the following by circling T (True) or F (False). Answers are given in the appendix.

1. Thoughts have no impact on emotional feelings.   T   F

2. To change negative thoughts, you must first find out exactly what you are predicting could happen, in as much detail as possible.   T   F

3. To jump to conclusions means to believe that positive events are never going to happen   T   F

4. A realistic odds judgment is made after considering all of the data and the evidence and is not based on how you feel.   T   F

5. It is better not to think about negative thoughts and instead to hope that they go away on their own.   T   F

6. Negative thoughts can occur so rapidly and automatically that you may not be aware of them.   T   F

SECTION 3   *Facing the Worst and Putting Things Into Perspective*

Seeing Things Out of Perspective

In the last section, we discussed jumping to conclusions. A second mistake that happens in our thinking whenever we are anxious is to blow things out of proportion or to think of situations as "insufferable" or "catastrophic" when, in actuality, they are not. Typical examples are: "If other people noticed that I was feeling very anxious or panicking, it would be terrible, and I could never face them again"; "It would be disastrous if I fainted"; "I couldn't cope with another panic attack"; or "It would be horrible if I felt anxious." If you stop to examine the situation realistically, usually it is not as awful as it seemed at first. For example, fainting, while extremely unlikely, is not such a terrible event. Fainting is actually an adaptive mechanism designed to reestablish the "balance" of bodily functions. Similarly, if another person noticed that you were anxious, the worst that might happen is that they would feel awkward, not knowing how to respond, or feel sympathy for you. Or, if someone did think you were weird, the worst that would happen is that they would not think of you in the way that you would like.

Another common catastrophic thought is, "Anything could happen the next time I panic. I don't know what it is, but it is going to be something bad." Again, this kind of negative thought generates anxiety. But if you examine the evidence and consider the worst that can happen, it is not as bad as you at first think.

Facing the Worst and Putting Things Back Into Perspective

Facing the worst and putting things back into perspective means to face whatever it is that is scaring you and, in so doing, to realize that it is not as bad as you at first thought. This is done by switching gears from focusing on "how bad it would be if . . ." to considering "ways of dealing with. . . ." When you come right down to it, everything is manageable to some degree. No matter how intense your fear is, you will survive. No matter how embarrassing the moment, it will pass. No matter how bad the event that you worry about, there is a way of getting through it.

In other words, there is always a way of coping, and it is always possible to get through even the worst situations.

For example, what if you actually did faint? What if others actually commented on the fact that you appeared shaky and nervous? What if you did scream and draw attention to yourself? What if you actually did walk out of a room because you felt trapped? Your first reaction to these questions might be something like "That would be awful or terrible," or, "I couldn't stand it." That is, however, blowing things out of proportion. When you really think about it, you will find that you have assumed them to be worse than they are.

In addition, there probably is a way of coping. Brainstorming ways of dealing with negative events (which is sometimes called *problem-solving*) is much more helpful than thinking only about how horrible it would be. For example, let us say that you fainted in front of a group of people. Think of ways of coping. What would you do? Picture what would happen to you as you woke up out of the faint; what might you do, what might you say, what would happen next? Maybe people would help you. Maybe you would ask for some water. Maybe you could say that you have not been feeling well lately, or that you have been suffering a severe flu, or that you were low on blood sugar, or even that you have been under a lot of stress—you can say whatever you want! Then what would you do? Maybe you would go home for the rest of the day. And what would you say to people the next day if they asked how you felt? And so on.

The basic point is that we can stand any misfortune that happens to us. It is only the belief that we cannot stand it that creates the anxiety. We can literally endure anything that befalls us until the day we die—and then, it does not matter anymore. Facing the worst and putting things back into perspective can be summed up in one phrase: So what? (The "So what?" strategy, however, does not apply to certain events, such as death, the loss of a loved one, or behaviors that conflict with strongly held religious beliefs or values.)

Here are two examples of putting things back into perspective.

Example 1

C: *I don't like to be in a crowd because if I panic, I might faint, and I don't know what would happen to me then.*

T: *Have you ever fainted before?*

C: *No*

T: *So, how likely do you think it is that you would faint?*

C: *Okay, maybe not very likely, but I know I'd have to leave, and that would be embarrassing.*

T: *Have you ever been embarrassed before?*

C: *Oh, yes.*

T: *Well, you're here, so I take it that you survived being embarrassed. How long does your embarrassment usually last?*

C: *Well, it's bad for a few minutes, then it kind of goes away. I don't know. Maybe it lasts a couple of hours in all.*

T: *Okay, so it's not very likely that you would faint, but you might leave, and that might be embarrassing, but embarrassment doesn't really last very long.*

Example 2

C: *I am worried that I might lose control and do something crazy, like yell and scream.*

T: *Aside from the very low likelihood of that happening (as we discussed before), let's face the worst and ask what is so bad about it. What would be so horrible about yelling and screaming?*

C: *I could never live it down.*

T: *Well, let's think it through. What are ways of coping?*

C: *Well, I guess the yelling and screaming would eventually stop.*

T: *That's right—at the very least, you would eventually exhaust yourself. What else?*

C: *Well, maybe I would explain to the people around me that I was having a really bad day, but that I would be okay. In other words, reassure them.*

T: *Good. What else?*

C: *Maybe I would just get away—find somewhere to calm down and reassure myself that the worst is over.*

T: *That's right. And maybe there are other things you could do, too.*

Your anxiety may increase as you begin to focus on these kinds of images and thoughts. However, the thoughts become less anxiety provoking the more often you face them. Only by facing them directly can you learn that the worst is not as bad as you first imagined. Remember, everything passes with time, and there is always a way of managing even the worst situation.

In summary, deal with times when you blow things out of proportion by (1) facing the worst; (2) realizing that even the worst situations pass with time and can be managed; and (3) thinking of ways of coping with the situation and with your feelings in the situation.

Go back to your list of Negative Thoughts from Section 2, and identify examples of where you were blowing things out of proportion. (You will know this if it feels like what you are worried about is catastrophic or beyond your coping abilities.) Then, face the worst, and consider ways of coping for each example by following the steps provided and completing each section of the Changing Your Perspective form as you go. You may photocopy this form from the book or download multiple copies at the Treatments *ThatWork*™ website (http://www.oup.com/us/ttw).

I.   Face head-on whatever it is that are most worried about happening.

II. Recognize that whatever it is you are worried about is not going to last forever and is survivable. (This does not, however, include events such as death, significant loss, or behaviors that conflict with strongly held religious beliefs or values.)

  ▪ Develop different ways of thinking, and record that next to the section titled "Will this pass and will I survive?"

  ▪ Remember—the goal in doing this is not positive thinking but *realistic* thinking.

  ▪ For example, if you believe that you would never emotionally recover from an embarrassing moment or from feeling afraid, think about the fact that these feelings are temporary, and realize that you would in fact recover.

  ▪ In general, the goal is to realize that you will be able to survive whatever happens to you and that whatever it is you are most worried about will not last forever.

III. Develop ways of coping

  ▪ Switch gears from focusing on "how bad it would be if a difficult situation happened" to considering "ways of dealing with a difficult situation." List actual coping steps.

Thinking Skills in General

Sometimes your negative thoughts will be based on just one mistake—either jumping to conclusions or blowing things out of proportion—in which case, you would deal with just that one. Sometimes both mistakes are pres-

Changing Your Perspective

Negative thought: _____

_____

_____

Will this pass, and will I survive? _____

_____

_____

_____

_____

_____

_____

Ways of coping:

_____

_____

_____

_____

_____

_____

ent, in which case, you would examine the evidence to generate realistic odds and alternative, evidence-based ways of thinking so that you do not jump to conclusions, as well as face the worst, realize that even bad situations pass with time and are manageable, and think of ways of coping with the situation and your feelings in the situation in order to put things back into perspective.

Do not be discouraged if this approach to thinking skills seems artificial at first. As with other skills in this program, learning to change your negative thoughts takes practice. With repetition, it will get easier, and the new ways of thinking will become more natural. Eventually, it will become so natural that you will not have to go through the entire process of finding negative thoughts and looking at the evidence or facing the worst—instead, you will automatically think in less negative ways.

Also, remember that the primary goal for thinking skills is *not* to eliminate anxiety. Instead, the thinking skills are intended to correct mistakes in your thinking so that you can continue to move forward and face the situations and things that make you anxious; eventually, your anxiety will subside.

Summary of Thinking Skills

The first step is to know the details of what you are most worried about happening in a specific situation.

For worries that involve *jumping to conclusions* (i.e., repeated worries about a negative event that rarely or never happens), the steps include the following:

1. Ask, "Has what I am most worried about come true?" (If traumatized, however, the question refers to the interval of time since the trauma.)

2. Consider mistaken reasons for why the worry continues.

3. Review all of the evidence.

4. Consider the realistic odds.

5. List different ways of thinking that are more evidenced based.

For worries that involve *blowing things out of proportion,* the steps for putting things into perspective include the following.

1. Face the worst as if it were actually happening, and realize that even the worst situation is survivable.

2. Switch from thinking about how bad it would be to steps of coping with the negative event if it were to happen.

Homework

✎ Continue recording your panic attacks and daily mood using the Panic Attack Record and Daily Mood Record. At the end of the week, add the number of panic attacks and average daily anxiety to your Progress Record.

✎ Practice Changing Your Perspective for each example of blowing things out of proportion from your list of Negative Thoughts.

✎ Practice either Changing Your Odds and/or Changing Your Perspective for any panic attacks that occur over this next week.

✎ After one week, continue on to Section 4.

Self-Assessment

Answer each of the following by circling T (True) or F (False). Answers are given in the appendix.

1. The fact that I have thoughts about being overwhelmed or collapsing means that these things actually are going to happen.   T   F

2. No one else has these kinds of thoughts. I must be really crazy.   T   F

3. Forcing myself to think about the worst will make me anxious initially, but the more I think about it and put things in perspective, the less anxious I will feel eventually.   T   F

4. Finding and changing negative thoughts is easy, and this process should not take much practice. T F

5. A panic attack will not continue forever. It is time limited and manageable. Even if I do nothing, it will pass. T F

SECTION 4   *Review of Thinking Skills and Dealing With Memories*

Review of Thinking Skills Practice

Have you been able to pin down your negative thoughts in a lot of detail and whenever you became anxious or panicky? Have you labeled the negative thoughts such as jumping to conclusions or seeing things out of perspective? Were you able to examine the evidence and put things back into perspective by looking at the realistic probabilities and facing the worst, realizing that difficult situations and emotions are time limited and that there always are ways of coping? Were you able to say, "So what"? It might feel artificial at first to always examine and change your thoughts. However, as you practice, this style of thinking will become more natural. It is the same as when we learn a new language: initially, it takes a lot of effort and seems unnatural, but with practice, it becomes more natural.

Keep in mind, also, that the goal of your work with your negative thoughts is not to get rid of anxiety or the physical symptoms immediately. Instead, the goal is to correct the mistaken thinking—the jumping to conclusions and the blowing things out of proportion—which contributes to the snowballing spiral of fear and anxiety. For example, let us say that you begin to feel dizzy and scared. You identify the negative thought as, "This dizziness makes me feel as if I am about to faint." You use your thinking skills by realizing that "I have felt dizzy many times before, and I have never fainted, so it is very unlikely that I will faint. The dizziness is just an uncomfortable symptom probably due to a change in my breathing or my anxiety level." Then, you notice that you are still feeling dizzy. The persistence of physical symptoms does *not* mean that your thinking skills have failed. Your new analysis that the feeling of dizziness is harmless is still accurate. Dizziness just may take some time to subside. Related to this, remember that some physical symptoms occur no matter how anxious or afraid you are. All of us have times when we feel off-balance, short of breath, lightheaded, trembly, or a racing heart. In other words, even if you use your thinking skills properly, you may still have occasions when you feel physical symptoms that remind you of panic attacks.

Also, watch out for the "don't worry, be happy" syndrome. For example, compare someone who says, "It will be okay, I'm fully in control, nothing bad will happen," to someone who says, "What am I afraid of? I'm afraid of fainting. How likely is it that I will faint, given the fact that I have felt this way so many times before and have never fainted? I know that I tend to jump to conclusions about the risk of fainting. The feelings will pass." The first person is trying for a quick fix, which does not really work in the long run. The second person is examining his or her thoughts and looking for new ways of thinking based on real evidence. This is what works in the long run.

Finally, remember that you are learning a new skill. Therefore, it takes time for the new ways of thinking to become more powerful than the old ways of thinking. In other words, "old habits die hard." For this reason, it is not unusual for negative thoughts to reappear despite previous successes in looking at the evidence and putting things back into perspective. Treat the old negative thoughts in the same way as you did the first time; that is, for each time a negative thought comes to mind, even if it is the same one time and time again, repeat the strategy of looking at the evidence, facing the worst, and putting things back into perspective. Repetition makes the new way of thinking stronger and more natural.

Dealing With Frightening Memories

Whenever a past event is given a lot of significance (such as when thought of as horrible), it is more easily remembered. In addition, the more frequently an event is remembered, the more likely it will be remembered again. Frightening memories then lead us to think of related future events as frightening also. Therefore, if you tend to think of the worst panic that you have ever had as a terrifying, horrific experience, something that you do not fully understand, and, in fact, it scares you just to think about it, then that memory probably contributes to your anxiety about future panics.

Many of our clients become less anxious and less on edge about the next panic attack after they learn to understand their past panics rather than just being horrified by them. This comes from forcing yourself to think about past panic attacks using a matter-of-fact approach.

To do this, first, recall the worst panic and, as clearly as you can, remember the context. This includes the people, the place, the sounds, the colors, the objects around you, and anything else. Imagine it as clearly as you can by placing yourself in the picture not as an observer, but as someone in the scene. Remember how you felt. You might become quite anxious or fearful as you think about that event. Statements such as, "I hate to even think about it," "I hope I never experience anything like that again," "I couldn't go through that again," "I'm sure I nearly died," or "I was so lucky to survive" are a good indicator of the importance of the next section.

Think about the worst panic again, particularly, the way you felt. Identify what, in retrospect, were the triggers for the panic: was it a physical symptom, was it a negative thought, was it a time you were under a lot of stress? How did you react? What was the first thing that happened? Did you have some negative thoughts, and did they produce more physical symptoms? Use a step-by-step analysis: Did you jump to any conclusions (e.g., did you think that you were going to die)? Did you blow things out of proportion (e.g., did you think that everyone would notice and think you were crazy)? What was the next thing that happened? Did you become more frightened? What did you do? Did you go to a hospital, or try to escape, call for help, or lie down? How did this add to the fear cycle? Furthermore, what was the actual end result? In other words, you did survive, and you did not die, lose control, or go crazy. Your goal is to think it through in a matter-of-fact manner, so that it becomes understandable. In other words, come to the realization that the reason you panicked is because, for example, you felt some unusual physical symptoms, had negative thoughts that something was terribly wrong, and these led you to become intensely afraid. Also, realize that, in the end, nothing was terribly wrong and that the worst that happened was that you became afraid.

Continue to repeat this exercise of rethinking through a worst panic attack until thinking about it no longer makes you feel anxious, until you have an understanding of why it happened; and until you realize that you did survive. We call this *processing* a past event, of which the goal is to have lessdisturbing memories about it and, therefore, to be less anxious about the same thing happening again in the future.

Homework

✎ Continue recording your panic attacks and daily mood using the Panic Attack Record and Daily Mood Record. At the end of the week, add the number of panic attacks and daily average anxiety to your Progress Record.

✎ Continue to practice either Changing Your Odds or Changing Your Perspective (or both) for any panic attacks that occur over this next week.

✎ Practice using a step-by-step analysis of your worst panic attack.

Self-Assessment

Answer each of the following by circling T (True) or F (False). Answers are given in the appendix.

1. To rate the odds of a negative event means to realize that negative events are always likely.   T   F

2. Thinking about ways of coping with worst-case scenarios should be done for all examples of jumping to conclusions.   T   F

3. Thinking skills are not intended to eliminate anxiety but rather are intended to help you deal with things that make your anxious.   T   F

4. Thinking back over the worst panic attack and realizing the sequence of events should be avoided at all cost.   T   F

Chapter 8 — *Facing Agoraphobia Situations*

Goals

- ■ To understand the value of facing agoraphobia situations

- ■ To learn how to optimally face agoraphobia situations

- ■ To review what is learned from facing agoraphobia situations

- ■ To continue to face agoraphobia situations

Completing this chapter will take a number of weeks (e.g., six weeks), although the actual amount of time will depend on the number of situations on your Hierarchy of Agoraphobia Situations and on the pace of your progress with those situations.

SECTION 1 — *Planning for and Practicing Facing Agoraphobia Situations*

Value of Directly Facing Agoraphobia Situations

Up until now, our focus has been upon coping with anxiety. Now, it is time to move into learning from direct experience. In many ways, direct experience is the most powerful way of learning. It is essential that you eventually repeatedly face and deal with all the situations on your hierarchy. By avoiding those situations, new learning is prevented; instead, fear and anxiety are reinforced. The more you avoid something, the more you will remain anxious about whatever it is you are avoiding. You may choose to involve a significant other in this phase of treatment, in which you will be directly facing the agoraphobia situations that make you anxious. If so, read chapter 9.

Sometimes people believe that they have already tried to face agoraphobia situations, without any success. As a result, they mistakenly judge that this treatment approach does not work. However, it is likely that previous unsuccessful attempts at facing the fear were not structured in exactly the right way. We review the possible reasons why it may not have worked in the past as a way to present the correct method of conducting exposure exercises.

Possibly, you believe that you practiced facing agoraphobia situations when, in fact, you did not. For example, being forced into a situation is not the same as setting up a specific task to practice over and over again. A one-time drive on the freeway to visit a sick family member in an emergency is not the same as practicing driving on the freeway three to four times a week in order to overcome a driving phobia. So, it is important not to confuse difficult or negative one-time experiences with truly facing your fear of agoraphobia situations.

Attempts to face agoraphobic situations may not have been done frequently enough, meaning that there was too much time between one practice to the next. For example, walking around a shopping mall once a month is much less helpful than walking around the mall once a week. Related to this is the possibility that the practice was not continued for long enough. For example, 90 minutes per day practicing being alone is much more helpful than just 5 minutes of practice per day. This is because a sufficient length of time is needed for new things to be learned. Facing your fear for brief periods of time decreases the chances of learning something new.

Most importantly, the practice may not have involved the right conditions. Repeatedly facing agoraphobia situations only works if you learn what is critical for you to learn. For example, if your fear of shopping malls is based on the notion that you will go insane if you spend more than 15 minutes in the mall, then the practice that will give you the critical learning is to shop for more than 15 minutes so that you learn that you do not lose your mind. Repeated practice for less than 15 minutes will not provide critical learning.

Perhaps you relied too much on superstitious objects, safety signals, safety behaviors, or distractions as you attempted to face agoraphobia situations.

Remember, these are unhelpful ways of coping because they interfere with corrective learning and contribute to anxiety in the long term.

Systematic, frequent, and lengthy practices under the conditions necessary for critical learning, without safety signals, superstitious objects, safety behaviors, or distraction, will be much more successful.

The practices with agoraphobia situations are intended to do three things:

1. Gather new information that will help you fully realize that what you are worried about happening is very unlikely to happen or never happens, that when you face the worst, it is not as bad as you first thought, and that there are ways of coping, even with difficult situations.

2. Let you learn that you can handle and survive the feelings of anxiety and fear.

3. Show you that you can accomplish the things that you have been avoiding.

Use of Medication

The use of medication has to be considered: particularly, medications that either block all of your feelings or medications that you rely on to reduce your fear in the moment (the latter include fast-acting medications, such as Xanax and Klonopin).

If medications are so potent that they block all feelings, then they may interfere with the benefits you can receive from actually facing your fear of agoraphobia situations. That is, some anxiety is very helpful—we learn more when we are anxious in comparison to when we are completely relaxed. So, if your anxiety and panic are completely blocked by medications, it may be helpful to talk with your prescriber about lowering the dosage of medication.

The second issue concerns the use of fast-acting medications. Initially, when you first face agoraphobia situations, you may feel the need for Xanax or Klonopin because those medications have been your usual coping tool. That is acceptable, as long as you eventually become comfortable enough so that you can face these situations without those medications. (We talk more about ways of reducing medications in chapter 11.)

Your Practice Facing an Agoraphobia Situation

Design of the Practice

Now it is time to design your practice with an agoraphobia situation. Choose the first item from your hierarchy, and go through the following steps.

I.   Identify what it is that you are most worried about happening in this situation. This is called the *Negative Thought.* This could be a concrete outcome, such as fainting, going insane, or having a heart attack, or it could be the idea that you cannot handle the anxiety associated with the situation.

II. Think about the best conditions in which to practice so that you can truly learn that your negative thoughts are unrealistic. These are called the *end goals.*

For example, if you believe that you could walk from one end of the mall to the other one time without fainting, but you are convinced that you would faint if you were to walk to the end and back again, then of course the best conditions for you to practice are to walk to the end and back again. Similarly, if you believe that you could walk into the mall for 10 minutes one time only but that to return into the mall three times would certainly cause you to faint, then of course the best conditions to practice will be to return to the mall three times. So, take into account how long you need to be in a situation or how many times you need to face the agoraphobia situation in order to learn that whatever you are most worried about either does not happen or that you can cope. At the same time, learning that your negative thoughts are unrealistic will require that you let go of all superstitious objects, safety signals, safety behaviors, or distractions. So, go back to your lists of Superstitious/Safety Signals and Safety Behaviors/Distractions from chapter 5, and plan for eventually practicing each agoraphobia situation without anything on those lists.

There is one possible exception to these objects, which is the cellular phone. In today's world, cell phones can sometimes be very helpful in the event of a true emergency. We recommend traveling without them only to learn that you will not die from a heart attack, faint, or be otherwise incapacitated if you do not have your cell phone on hand. At the same time, we recognize that cell phones can be valuable tools if your car breaks down.

III. Choose either to gradually work up to the end goals or to go directly to the end goals.

For example, if the end goal is to walk around the mall for one hour alone (because that is the point at which you currently are sure that you will faint if you are alone), you may start by completing 20 minutes with a friend and then 20 minutes alone; 40 minutes with a friend and then 40 minutes alone; and 60 minutes with a friend and then 60 minutes alone. Or, you could go straight to doing the full 60 minutes alone. *Today's goals* are the conditions in which you will practice on a given day as you work toward your end goals.

An example is shown here.

IV. Use your thinking skills.

In preparation for the practice, ask yourself the following.
- Has what you are most worried about ever happened? (If it has not or rarely has, then you are jumping to conclusions?)

Facing Agoraphobia Situations

Situation: *Drive on surface streets.*

Negative Thought (i.e., whatever it is you are most worried about happening): *I will lose control of the car and drive into oncoming traffic.*

End Goal: *Drive one hour alone.*

Today's Goal: *Drive 20 minutes with husband.*

Figure 8.1.
Example of Part of Completed Facing Agoraphobia Situations Form

Facing Agoraphobia Situations

Negative Thought: _I will lose control of the car and drive into oncoming traffic._

How many times has it happened? _None._

What is the evidence? _Even though I feel numb and weak, I can still move my arms and legs, and I can still think, so I probably can control the car._

What are the real odds? (0–100): _Zero._

Ways of coping: _I will breathe calmly and remind myself that I am in control._

Figure 8.2.

Example of Part of Completed Facing Agoraphobia Situations Form Using Thinking Skills

■ What is the worst that can happen, and how would you cope with it? (If the worst feels unbearable, and you feel as if you could not cope, then you are blowing things out of proportion.)

■ Then:

    a. look at all the evidence;

    b. consider the real odds;

    c. realize that the worst is probably not as bad as you first thought; and

    d. think of ways of coping.

An example of using these thinking skills is shown above.

This situation is to be practiced at least three times over the next week (either going straight to your end goals or gradually working up to your end goals across each practice). If your situation is very brief (e.g., riding four floors on an elevator), then continue practicing over and over again on a given day until you spend about an hour practicing.

You will continue to practice a given situation for the number of days necessary for your maximum anxiety level to reduce to 2 or less. Whether your level of anxiety decreases or not within a given practice is not important; what is more important is that over each day of practice, the level of anxiety eventually decreases. Now, we will consider ways of making the practice as effective as possible.

Moment of Fear

If you become afraid or nervous during the practice, use your breathing and thinking skills to help you continue to move forward and complete the practice. First, practice breathing by doing the following.

- Focus your attention on breathing and counting.

- Count for one second, inhale for two seconds, think the word "relax" for one second, and exhale for two seconds.

- Expand your stomach when you breathe in, and deflate your stomach when you breathe out, keeping your chest relatively still, without taking big breaths.

- Count up to 10 and back to one, one time.

Then, ask yourself the following key questions, so that you can use your thinking skills.

- What is it that I am most worried about happening?

- What are the real chances of that happening?

- What will I do to cope with and manage this situation?

Escape

If, while you are doing your practice, you feel as if you absolutely have to leave because your fear and anxiety are so intense, the best strategy is to leave the situation *temporarily* and, after using your skills, return to the situation again. Here are some examples.

- If you are driving on the freeway, pull off the freeway and find a place to stop. Practice your breathing skills, and ask yourself the same key questions listed above to help you use your thinking skills. Then, get back on the freeway.

- If you are in a shopping mall, find a place to sit down near the exit or just outside the mall and, after you have used your breathing and thinking skills, return back into the shopping mall.

The number-one rule is that if you escape from a situation and do not return to it, you will end up back where you started and will not make progress. So, you must always return to the situation.

After the Practice

After the practice is completed;

- rate whether what you were most worried about occurred or not (yes or no);

- rate your level of maximal anxiety during the practice on a 0–10-point scale, where 0 = no anxiety and 10 = extreme anxiety.

Think about what happened, your accomplishments, and what you might do differently next time. Watch out for unhealthy self-criticism. Remember, if you felt anxious as you faced the situation, that is fine—in fact, it is expected, and it is good. Learning is helped by anxiety, especially since two of the most critical things to learn are that anxiety is not harmful and that you can handle anxiety. Also, remember that whether your anxiety decreases within a given practice is not so important; more important is that eventually, over repetitions of days of practice, the anxiety decreases. Finally, remember what you actually accomplished. For example, it is much more helpful to reward yourself for having driven two miles on the freeway than to criticize yourself for not having driven further. It is the accomplishments that are most important, no matter how small the accomplishment may seem to be.

Homework

- Continue recording your panic attacks and daily mood using the Panic Attack Record and Daily Mood Record. At the end of the week, add the number of panic attacks and daily average of anxiety to your Progress Record.

- Read chapter 9 over the next week to learn about involving family or friends.

- Practice Changing Your Odds and/or Changing Your Perspective for any panic attacks that occur over this next week.

- Practice facing an agoraphobia situation at least three times this week. You may practice more than one situation from your hierarchy at one time.

- Continue on to section 2 after you have practiced facing agoraphobia situations at least 3 times.

Facing Agoraphobia Situations

Date: _____

Situation: _____

_____

_____

End Goals (excluding superstitious objects, safety signals, safety behaviors, and distractions): _____

_____

_____

Today's Goals: _____

_____

_____

Negative Thought (i.e., whatever it is you are most worried about happening): _____

_____

_____

How many times has it happened? _____

What is the evidence? _____

_____

What are the real odds? (0–100) _____

Ways of coping: _____

_____

_____

_____

Did what I most worried about occur? (Yes/No) _____

Maximal anxiety (0–10): _____

```
0 ------- 1 ------- 2 ------- 3 ------- 4 ------- 5 ------- 6 ------- 7 ------- 8 ------- 9 ------- 10
   None           Mild          Moderate          Strong          Extreme
```

Answer each of the following by circling T (True) or F (False). Answers are given in the appendix.

1. It is essential that you do not think about your feelings when you face agoraphobia situations.   T   F

2. Occasional practice with agoraphobia situations is acceptable.   T   F

3. Practice each agoraphobia situation only once.   T   F

4. Experiencing anxiety or fear when you are in the agoraphobia situation means that you have failed   T   F

5. It is essential to eventually practice facing the agoraphobia situation enough times and for long enough, and without superstitious objects, safety signals, safety behaviors, or distractions, so that something new can be learned.   T   F

6. The goal of facing agoraphobia situations is to learn that whatever you are most worried about rarely happens or never happens; that there is a way of coping with the worst; and that you can handle fear and anxiety and accomplish something you have been avoiding.   T   F

SECTION 2   *Review and Continued Planning and Practice Facing Agoraphobia Situations*

Review of Practicing Facing Agoraphobia Situations

What Did You Learn?

Did the practices help you to realize that you had been mistakenly jumping to conclusions and/or blowing things out of proportion? Did your practices help you to realize that you can handle fear and anxiety? Did your practices help you to realize that you can accomplish things that you have been avoiding? Of course, these three goals will become more fully realized with continued and repeated practice.

Dealing With Escapes

Sometimes anxiety feels overwhelming, and you may choose to escape from the situation without returning to it the same day. Treat this as a learning experience, and if you did escape, spend some time now thinking about why.

- What kind of symptoms did you feel?

- What kind of negative thoughts were going through your mind?

- What were you anticipating had you continued with the activity?

You were probably jumping to conclusions and/or blowing things out of proportion, in which case, go back to your thinking skills by looking at the evidence and putting things back into perspective.

Also, remember that these practices are not supposed to be associated with zero anxiety or fear. That is, you should feel anxious at first, or else there would be no need to do them at all. In fact, some anxiety is critical, as it helps you to learn that the feelings of fear and anxiety are not dangerous in and of themselves and can be handled. Furthermore, sometimes the anxiety increases at first before it decreases, because you are facing things that you have been avoiding. However, with repeated practice, the anxiety will eventually decrease.

If your level of anxiety remains high after many repetitions of practicing with the same situation, it may be that you are putting too much focus on trying to prevent yourself from feeling anxious in the situation instead of accepting the anxiety and focusing on your breathing and thinking skills to help you face the situation.

Continuing to Plan for and Practice Facing Agoraphobia Situations

Choose the next item from your Hierarchy of Agoraphobia Situations, and apply the same principles as described in section 1. Continue doing this for as long as it takes for you to complete all of the items from your hierarchy.

Context of First Panic Attack

The contexts in which first panic attacks are experienced are likely to carry special significance. For example, let us say that your discomfort about driving began with a panic attack while driving home alone at night to an empty house. After that, fears of driving expanded to driving in the day, on surface streets and on freeways. In addition to facing your fear of driving during the day and night, on surface streets and on freeways, it will be particularly important to face your fears of driving under the same conditions in which the first panic occurred; that is, to face the situation of driving home alone at night to an empty house. Similarly, let us say that your first panic attack occurred in a movie theater that was crowded and hot, and when you were suffering from a cold. It would be particularly helpful to face your fears of movie theaters under similar conditions of being crowded, hot, and when you are feeling congested or experiencing other cold symptoms.

Homework

✎ Continue recording your panic attacks and daily mood using the Panic Attack Record and Daily Mood Record, and at the end of each week, complete your Progress Record.

✎ Practice Changing Your Odds and/or Changing Your Perspective for any panic attacks that occur over this next week.

✎ Practice facing an agoraphobia situation at least three times a week, continuing until you have practiced all of the items from your hierarchy. You may practice more than one situation from your hierarchy at one time.

✎ Consider ways to practice facing agoraphobia situations in the context of your first panic attack.

✎ Continue to section 3 once you have completed at least one half of your Hierarchy of Agoraphobia Situations or when you have reached Week 10 of the treatment program.

Facing Physical Symptoms in Agoraphobia Situations

It is conceivable (although unlikely) that you could face all of your agoraphobia situations without ever experiencing a physical symptom that normally distresses you. Think of a woman who is concerned about driving, especially when her arms feel weak because she mistakenly thinks that the weakness means that she is about to lose control of the car. What would happen if she faced the situation of driving the freeways each day without ever feeling weakness in her arms? That would be okay, as long as she never felt the weakness ever again. But that is an unlikely scenario. So, it is best to be prepared for the physical symptoms in agoraphobia situations.

You would probably agree that the situations would be easier to deal with if you were guaranteed never to feel the physical symptoms. But that is unrealistic, especially if you are at all anxious about the situation; as we know, anxiety brings about symptoms in and of itself. In addition, some symptoms will occur regardless of your anxiety, such as the rise in body temperature which may occur in a crowded shopping area, or the eyestrain that may occur due to driving, or the stomach fullness that might occur after eating a meal in a restaurant. It is better to face everything—the symptoms and the situation—rather than to wish that the symptoms will never occur.

By this time in the program, you should have completed much of chapter 10, in which you learn to face physical symptoms that make you anxious. Now, it is time to incorporate your work from chapter 10 and accept and even exaggerate the physical symptoms in your practices with agoraphobia situations.

Entering a situation with the *intention* of having physical symptoms is evidence that you do not fear the symptoms. On the other hand, entering a situation with the hope that physical symptoms do not develop is evidence that you still fear the symptoms. There are many ways in which to purposely bring on the physical symptoms as you face different situations:

■ driving your car with the heater on and windows rolled up (*heat*);

■ wearing woolen clothes, jackets, or turtlenecks (*heat*);

- looking behind yourself quickly while walking (*dizziness, loss of balance*);

- drinking coffee (*racy feelings*);

- eating pasta or other heavy foods (*fullness of stomach*);

- walking up flights of stairs (*racing or pounding heart*);

- not wearing sunglasses on a sunny day (*eye fatigue*);

- wearing a tie or scarf (*tightness around the throat*).

So, follow the next steps to design your next practice, using the Facing Symptoms and Agoraphobia Situations form.

1. Identify the situation from your hierarchy that you will practice. It may be a new item that you have not yet practiced; or, if you have practiced all items on your hierarchy, then practice the item rated with the highest anxiety rating again.

2. Choose a symptom that you will intensify, and decide how and when you will deliberately produce that symptom as you deal with your anxious situation. This is called *symptom exaggeration.*

3. Think about the best conditions to practice in so that you can truly learn that your negative thoughts are unrealistic. These are called the *end goals.* Remember to exclude superstitious objects, safety signals, safety behaviors, and distractions.

4. Choose to either gradually work up to the end goals or go directly to the end goals. If you choose a gradual approach, your today's goals will be different from the end goals.

5. Identify what it is that you are most worried about happening in this situation while experiencing the symptoms. This is called *negative thought.*

6. Then apply your thinking skills to the negative thought. (How many times has it happened? What is the evidence? What are the real odds? What are some ways of coping?)

7. After the practice, record whether what you were most worried about occurred, and record your maximal anxiety.

Facing Symptoms and Agoraphobia Situations

Date: _____

Situation: _____

_____

_____

Symptom Exaggeration: _____

_____

End Goals (excluding superstitious objects, safety signals, safety behaviors, and distractions):_____

_____

_____

Today's Goals:_____

_____

_____

Negative Thought (i.e., whatever it is you are most worried about happening, with the symptoms in the situation):

_____

_____

How many times has it happened? _____

What is the evidence? _____

_____

_____

What are the real odds? (0–100) _____

Ways of coping: _____

_____

_____

_____

Did what I most worried about occur? (Yes/No) _____

Maximal anxiety (0–10): _____

```
0------1------2------3------4------5------6------7------8------9------10
None        Mild       Moderate        Strong       Extreme
```

✎ Continue recording your panic attacks and daily mood using the Panic Attack Record and Daily Mood Record. At the end of the week, add the number of panic attacks and daily average anxiety to your Progress Record.

✎ Use Changing Your Odds and/or Changing Your Perspective for any panic attacks that occur over this next week.

✎ Practice facing an agoraphobia situation and the symptoms in that situation at least three times this week. You may practice more than one situation from your hierarchy at one time. Continue this practice until you have repeated all of the situations from your Hierarchy of Agoraphobia Situations with all of the symptoms that make you anxious enough times, so that your maximum anxiety is no greater than a score of 2.

✎ Once you have completed these practices and all of the material in chapter 10, then move to the final phase of the treatment by reading chapter 11, section 2, and chapter 12.

Chapter 9   *Involving Others*

Goals

- Understand reasons for including others

- Plan effective ways for including others

  In this chapter, we present ways for incorporating others, such as husbands, wives, family, or friends, to help you confront your fears of agoraphobia situations. You may skip this section if there are no others who can assist you in this endeavor or if you prefer to work alone.

Why Seek the Help of Someone Else?

Research suggests that involving spouses, life partners, family, or friends in the therapy process facilitates a pattern of continuing improvement, especially after formal therapy is over. Therefore, we recommend that you seek the aid of a family member, friend, life partner, or spouse whom you think would be willing to help you.

It makes sense when you think about it.

First, agoraphobic behavior can impact others in your life. By avoiding situations, certain tasks or chores that used to be yours may need to be taken over by others. Although the other person may be doing this in order to help you out, by taking over your normal activities, they may inadvertently reinforce your fear and avoidance. For example, let us say that to help you with your fear of driving and waiting in lines, your husband now stops at the store on the way home from work to pick up the groceries. In turn, because you do not drive or stand in lines, you do not have the chance to learn to be less afraid of those situations. Furthermore, you may develop a sort of dependence on your husband. That is, you rely on him more and more to take you places and to do the things that you used to do on your own. As you might guess, such dependence brings a whole lot of other problems with it—sometimes resentment on both sides and arguments—all because your husband was initially trying to help you out and you thought that you were doing the right thing. Awareness of these patterns is the first step to change.

Another possibility is that your spouse, life partner, family member, or friend may inadvertently reinforce your fear and avoidance by giving a lot of attention to you when you are afraid. If the attention you receive (which is something we all like to receive) is stronger when you are afraid than when you are not afraid, then it makes sense that your fear may become motivated by attention from your spouse or life partner. Of course, you might not be fully aware of this pattern, and it might be subconscious. This is because we all tend to respond to attention by increasing the behavior that produced the attention in the first place. So, let us say that your girlfriend hugs you especially long, or is especially caring for you, when you are anxious or that an argument is immediately forgotten when she learns that you are experiencing distress; it makes sense that, in some way, you learn that such positive attention can be obtained from being anxious. This is certainly not to say that all of your anxiety is designed to receive positive rewards; the cost of anxiety almost always outweighs the benefits. Nevertheless, this type of reinforcement can be a contributing factor, and therefore, one that should be modified. It is even possible for your significant other to find your dependence on him or her as reinforcing for them, so that in the end, he or she takes over more and more of your responsibilities.

Another possibility is that, due to their lack of understanding of the nature of panic attacks and agoraphobia, a concerned husband, wife, parent, or friend could exacerbate your own fears by overreacting to or by magnifying your panic symptoms. For example, a reaction from them of "Oh, my, we better go to the hospital as soon as possible" when you tell them that you feel as if you are about to faint might only serve to increase your own distress. Again, awareness of these patterns is the first step to change.

At the other end of the scale, your significant other may react to your difficulties with anger, frustration, lack of understanding, and nonsupport. In some ways, this is understandable, since your spouse, life partner, family member, or friend may feel that they have to take on responsibilities and chores that they really do not want to do or that they never expected to do. For someone who already has a busy schedule, taking on extra tasks can be a burden. This situation can be exacerbated when the significant other does not fully understand the nature of your problem. They may even make accusations that your problem is not real, that it is all in your head. Having an unsupportive or an accusing partner will add to your background stress and, in turn, make your progress through the treatments in this workbook a little slower and more difficult. Under these conditions, it is helpful to give the significant other a description of the nature of panic and agoraphobia and of how they are treated.

So, as you can see, a balance needs to be achieved between an overly dependent and reinforcing relationship with significant others and being shunned and accused by significant others. Incorporating their help in your progress to recovery is a way of achieving the right balance. By having them involved in your therapy, the significant other (from now on, called the *helper* or the *coach*) can become an aid, so that the two of you can work as a problem-solving team in applying all of the principles outlined in this workbook.

Ways for Your Helper to Understand

Your helper can learn about panic and agoraphobia by reading this workbook, by having a mental health professional explain things to them, or by asking you to explain things to them in as objective a way as possible. The latter is probably the most difficult, since strong emotions may have already been built up between the two of you regarding your panic and agoraphobia and their impact on your relationship.

Of course, the helper must have some motivation or willingness to understand and/or help out. Unfortunately, some people may be unwilling, although they may become interested and willing as they see you making progress. The best you can do is to suggest that they either read the workbook or talk to a mental health professional so as to better understand what you are going through. The fact that change would help them, as well as you, is another important concept to convey to your helper. In other words, your relationship will most likely get better when your panic and agoraphobia lessen.

The rest of this chapter proceeds as if your significant other has agreed to learn more and become a part of your recovery. In particular, this means that they become a kind of coach or aid when you face agoraphobia situations.

Preparation for the two of you to work as a team so as to overcome your panic and agoraphobia involves several steps.

The helper should learn about panic and agoraphobia. We recommend that your spouse, life partner, friend, or family member read this workbook. Along with this information is the understanding that your panic and agoraphobia are not consciously intentional and that this is not a problem that is "all in your head" or that "everything would be all right if you just pulled yourself together."

It is important that you recognize the way in which your helper's life has been impacted as the two of you have worked to accommodate agoraphobia. This means having a discussion with your helper and listing the areas of his or her life that have changed as a result of this problem. Of course, the goal of treatment is to alleviate your own distress, as well as any stress that it has placed on your helper. Joint recognition of problem areas is a good way to begin a process of change as a team.

Next, in continuing your discussion with your helper, it is helpful to identify which of their behaviors might reinforce your fear and avoidance, albeit inadvertently. Brainstorm together to identify the reinforcements. In particular, discuss whether your helper gives you the most positive attention at times when you are anxious, as opposed to when you are relatively relaxed. Also, identify which chores or tasks he or she has taken over that used to be yours. Finally, identify ways in which your helper might magnify your physical symptoms by overreacting to them. Reading the beginning section of this chapter might help coaches to realize how their own behaviors could be inadvertently maintaining their loved one's distress.

The next step is for your helper to learn about ways of overcoming panic and agoraphobia. In other words, they should understand the breathing and thinking skills for helping you to face agoraphobia situations. Along with this, your helper is to be discouraged from magnifying the experience of panic, such as believing that you are at risk for dying if your heart rate speeds up. Instead, they will begin to help you to use your thinking skills when you are anxious. At the same time, they are encouraged to be supportive and patient, since progress is rarely always smooth, ups and downs occur, and progress is dependent on a great deal of effort and persistence.

Helpers can become familiar with the thinking skills by reading the relevant sections of the workbook and by prompting you to use your thinking skills in preparation for each time you face agoraphobia situations. In this way, your helper can provide an objective focus that might be helpful to you when examining the evidence and developing alternatives.

Ways to Communicate

The next step in preparing to face agoraphobia situations with the direct help of your friend, family member, or life partner is to consider how to communicate when you are in the midst of feeling very anxious. Sometimes, we say things that we do not mean or in ways that we do not intend when feeling distressed. For that reason, it is useful to rehearse the most constructive type of communication before you and your helper head off to face agoraphobia situations.

We recommend that you use a 0–10-point rating system to communicate with each other about your own level of anxiety or distress as a way of diminishing the awkwardness associated with discussion of your feelings, especially in public situations. Furthermore, using a number scale helps to keep you on the track of being objective as opposed to distracting from how you are feeling or, on the other hand, being too subjective. It is much more effective to tell your helper that your anxiety level is a 6 instead of saying "I feel terrible." Similarly, it is much more effective for your helper to ask for a number rating than to ask, "How bad you are feeling?"

Of course, you may prefer not to let your helper know how anxious you are feeling at all, for reasons of embarrassment or attempts to avoid your anxiety due to the concern that your anxiety will intensify if you talk about it. Remember, attempts to distract from or avoid your anxiety are not helpful in the long run—it is much better to maintain an objective awareness of your reactions. The initial discomfort and embarrassment about discussing your anxiety with your helper will most likely reduce as the two of you become more familiar with discussing anxiety and its management.

Also, significant others should attempt to be neither too insensitive nor too pushy. For example, they may presume to know how anxious you feel or what is going through your mind without asking for confirmation from you. Alternatively, they may become angry or frustrated if you avoid or escape from a situation. Joint discussion in advance about how the helper can best react should you show hesitation or withdrawal is the best way to prevent negative communication during exposure. So, again, take on the issue as a team. Discuss what each person will do if you become very afraid or express an urge to leave. The two of you might decide to use keywords to communicate crucial concepts, especially if in public. For example, consider the following scenario.

YOU: *My anxiety is strong—at a 6, I want to leave.*

HELPER: *Thoughts?*

YOU: *The same old thing—I'm hot and sweaty, and I think I'm going to faint.*

HELPER: *Jumping to conclusions?*

YOU: *Yes—but the feelings are stronger than usual.*

HELPER: *How many times?*

YOU: *I know—I've never fainted.*

HELPER: *Sit?*

YOU: *Yes, let's sit down so that I can think about this.*

As you can see, the helper was using a few keywords that the couple had worked out beforehand, to prompt the individual suffering from anxiety look at the evidence and develop a coping strategy of sitting down versus escaping the situation.

Here is another example.

YOU: *I am terrified.*

HELPER: *Number?*

YOU: *It's a 7—I feel like I can't breathe.*

HELPER : *It's a feeling—is it true that you cannot breathe?*

YOU: *I know—I am getting enough air, but it's really difficult.*

HELPER: *Slow breathing?*

Here is yet another example.

> YOU: *I don't want to practice today—I am really tired. It's too hard, and I'm worn out.*

> HELPER: *What were you planning to do today?*

> YOU: *To go back to the bank lines. The same one I went to on Monday. I just don't feel up to it today.*

> HELPER: *I know it's hard, but it's helping—you can go places that used to be almost impossible for you.*

> YOU: *Yes—but I just need a rest.*

> HELPER: *Are you making any negative predictions about what could happen in the bank line because of the way you are feeling?*

> YOU: *Probably. I think that I really would pass out because I am so tired.*

> HELPER: *Okay—what is the evidence?*

> YOU: *I know . . . none. Okay, I will go.*

Support from the helper is important also. Support means recognizing attempts you make to overcome your fear and avoidance and reinforcing these attempts. This may differ from the usual pattern of reinforcement, which is to give most attention to you when you are in distress. Occasionally, your own success can seem deflated if the significant other in your life does not appreciate how hard you have worked or what a major accomplishment it is for you to initiate an activity that you have been avoiding for a long time. Let us say that you have been wanting to go out to dinner at a restaurant with your partner, something that the both of you used to really enjoy. Finally, you feel ready, and so you mention it to your significant other when he or she comes home from work. However, you partner is tired and refuses to go, suggesting that perhaps you do so another night. While it is understandable that your companion might be tired and not in your mindset at that moment, it is helpful if your partner realizes the significance of your initiative and reinforces your progress by agreeing to eat out, despite personal tiredness. On the other hand, it is also important for you to understand that your significant other may not always be as supportive as you would like because of his or her own troubles and concerns.

So with all of this information in mind, you can now proceed to include your helper as a coach when you face agoraphobia situations. The helper may be a coach by discussing the task before you attempt it and after it is over, prompting you to use your thinking skills and breathing, and helping you to evaluate your accomplishments objectively. Also, a coach can accompany you on the task. However, remember that if your helper accompanies you, she or he could become a safety signal. Therefore, it is essential that, eventually, you are able to face the situation on your own, without your spouse, life partner, friend, or family member. An example of how to wean yourself away from your helper gradually follows.

- Drive I-90 five exits, with your coach as the driver.

- Drive I-90 five exits, with your coach as the passenger.

- Drive I-90 five exits, with your coach in a different car, one car in front of you.

- Drive I-90 five exits, with your coach in a different car, two cars behind you.

- Drive I-90 five exits, with your coach in a different car, one half a mile behind you.

- Drive I-90 five exits, meeting your coach at a destination point.

- Drive I-90 five exits, without the help of your coach.

Homework

Return to chapter 8, and continue with planning for and practicing facing agoraphobia situations, either with or without the assistance of your helper.

Answer each of the following by circling T (True) or F (False). Answers are given in the appendix.

1. Family members or friends should never be involved in your treatment, as they will only contribute to the pressure for you to get better.   T   F

2. It is possible for your agoraphobia to be reinforced by attention from your family or friends or by having them take over your responsibilities.   T   F

3. If you do have a helper as you face agoraphobia situations, that person should read this workbook, think about the ways in which his or her life has been influenced by your agoraphobia, how he or she may have reinforced your agoraphobia, and learn the breathing and thinking skills.   T   F

4. In the midst of anxiety, it is better not to communicate with your helper.   T   F

5. Make sure the coach is always with you and that you are never left alone when you face agoraphobia situations.   T   F

Chapter 10   *Facing Physical Symptoms*

Goals

■ To understand the value of facing physical symptoms

■ To learn how to optimally face physical symptoms

■ To review what is learned from facing physical symptoms

■ To continue to face physical symptoms and activities

Completing this chapter will take a number of weeks (e.g., six weeks), although the actual amount of time will depend on the number of symptoms and activities that make you anxious and on the pace of your progress with those symptoms and activities.

SECTION 1   *Facing Physical Symptoms*

Face the Physical Symptoms: Why?

As you know by the now, fear of physical symptoms is central to panic disorder. You have been learning to change what you think about the physical symptoms. Now we will face the physical symptoms directly so that you can learn that the symptoms are not harmful; that you can handle the symptoms and the anxiety; and that, eventually, the anxiety about the physical symptoms will decrease. We have discussed how being afraid of physical symptoms leads to more physical symptoms, since the symptoms are the natural result of anxiety and fear. This is part of the panic cycle.

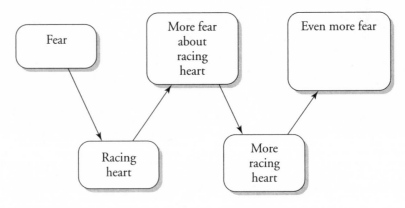

Figure 10.1.
Panic Cycle

As already mentioned, the reasons why fears of physical symptoms persist include:

- *avoidance behaviors* (e.g., doing whatever you can to get rid of the symptoms or avoiding places where you expect the symptoms to arise);

- *mistaken beliefs* (e.g., that the physical symptoms mean you are going to die, lose control, or go insane);

- *interoceptive conditioning,* where your body has become highly sensitive to the physical feelings of the beginnings of a panic attack.

The goal of this part of treatment is to help you directly face the physical symptoms that make you anxious (i.e., decrease avoidance), replace your mistaken beliefs with more realistic thinking, and interrupt the conditioning. To do this, we first identify which physical symptoms make you feel anxious, using a series of exercises that bring on symptoms similar to those that are typical of anxiety and panic. Next, we repeat the exercises that produce the symptoms enough times and in just the right way so that you learn that the symptoms are not harmful, that you can handle them, and that you can break the conditioning.

What normally happens in your day-to day-life is probably very different— you probably do everything possible to get rid of the physical symptoms, such as lie down, distract yourself by getting engaged in other activities, leave wherever you are, and so on. These actions are really avoidances, and they prevent you from learning that the symptoms are not harmful. So, we will do the opposite of what you normally do.

First, though, we would like to make a note about medical issues before we continue. Most of the symptom exercises are relatively mild in intensity. You are not being asked to run a marathon. However, they may be too intense for persons with certain medical conditions, which is one of the reasons why we always recommend that a medical evaluation be conducted if you have not had one in the last 12 months. If you do suffer from a medical condition (e.g., epilepsy, high blood pressure) alongside panic disorder, we recommend that you undertake these symptom-induction exercises under the guidance of your medical doctor. For example, have your doctor look at the list of symptom exercises and ask the doctor to indicate which ones are okay for you to do. Similarly, asthmatic sufferers should obtain medical clearance for these exercises, as should women who are pregnant.

Symptom Assessment

Here is the list of exercises.

1. Run in place, lifting your knees up as high as you can, for up two minutes, to produce racing heart and shortness of breath.

2. Spin around and around for up to one minute. If you have a chair that swivels, such as a desk chair, this is ideal. Otherwise, stand up and turn around quickly (about one turn every three seconds) to make yourself dizzy. Be near a soft chair or couch to sit on after one minute is up. This will produce dizziness and, perhaps, nausea as well.

3. Overbreathe for up to one minute—that is, breathe deeply and fast, using a lot of force, as if you were blowing up a balloon. Sit as you do this. This exercise produces unreality, shortness of breath, tingling, cold or hot feelings, dizziness or headache, and other symptoms. In fact, you have already done this exercise as part of chapter 6 when evaluating the role of overbreathing in your panic attacks. (*Do not do this exercise if you have epilepsy, seizures, or cardiopulmonary diseases.*)

4. Breathe through a drinking straw for up to 2 minutes. This will produce the feeling of not getting enough air.

5. Stare at yourself in a mirror for up two minutes. Stare as hard as you can to produce feelings of unreality.

6. Place your head between your legs for 30 seconds, and then sit up quickly, in order to produce feelings of lightheadedness or a sense of blood rushing away from your head.

7. Tense every part of your body, without causing pain, for up to one minute. Tense your arms, legs, stomach, back, shoulders, face—everything. This will produce feelings of muscle tension, weakness, and trembling.

After each exercise, you will do the following.

■ List all of the symptoms you felt.

■ Rate your anxiety about the symptoms on a 0–10 scale (where 0 = none at all, 5 = moderate, and 10 = extreme).

■ Rate how similar the symptoms are to the ones you would feel in a natural panic attack on a 0–10 scale (where 0 = not at all similar, and 10 = exactly the same).

Now, go ahead and attempt each exercise, and complete the Symptom Assessment form on page 157.

Here are Jill's responses to each of the standard exercises.

1. Running in place: Jill stopped this one after 45 seconds.

   "I feel like I have to stop—my heart is beating fast, and I feel sweaty and out of breath. Usually, I try to avoid doing any exercise." Jill rated this procedure as producing symptoms that were very intense (8), very similar to what she felt during her panic attacks (7), and, initially, that made her feel quite anxious (6).

2. Spinning: Jill stopped this after 30 seconds.

   "Boy, I feel really dizzy. The room is spinning—I am spinning. And my heart is racing, and I feel sweaty. It's calming down now." These symptoms were very intense (9), similar to those she felt when she panicked (7), and they caused some anxiety (5).

3. Hyperventilation: Jill stopped after 25 seconds.

   "I feel really hot and sweaty, tingly in my face, lightheaded, and like I need to take a deep breath." Again, this procedure produced symp-

Symptom Assessment

0 ------- 1 ------- 2 ------- 3 ------- 4 ------- 5 ------- 6 ------- 7 ------- 8 ------- 9 ------- 10

| None | Mild | Moderate | Strong | Extreme |

Exercise	Symptoms	Anxiety Level 1–10	Similarity 1–10
Run in place	_____	_____	_____
	_____		
Spinning	_____	_____	_____
	_____		
Overbreathing	_____	_____	_____
	_____		
Drinking-straw breathing	_____	_____	_____
	_____		
Stare at self in mirror	_____	_____	_____
	_____		
Lift head quickly	_____	_____	_____
	_____		
Tense body	_____	_____	_____
	_____		
Other	_____	_____	_____
	_____		
Other	_____	_____	_____
	_____		

toms that Jill rated as being very intense (9), similar to her natural panics (7), and that made her feel very anxious (8).

4. Drinking-straw breathing: Jill stopped after 35 seconds.

   "I feel like I can't keep going, I have to take a deep breath."

Jill rated the symptoms as strong (6), quite similar to her panic-symptoms (4), and making her feel somewhat anxious (5).

5. Staring at herself in the mirror.

   "This is weird. It feels a bit like the spacey feelings I get when I'm just coming out of a panic attack. I don't like this at all." Jill rated the symptoms as being moderate (5), fairly similar to her panic symptoms (4), and causing some anxiety (4).

6. Head lift.

   "I feel a little dizzy—and lightheaded. This was not much at all." She did not report any fear (0) or much similarity (2), and she rated the symptom intensity as being quite mild (2).

7. Body tension.

   "I feel a little shaky and trembly and weak." While the symptoms were quite intense for Jill (6), she did not rate them as very produc-tive of anxiety (1), and she rated the similarity as being low (1).

Now, look at your own ratings on the Symptom Assessment form. Star (*) the exercises that produced symptoms you rated as at least 2 on the 0–10 scale of similarity. Next, rank the starred exercises in order of the level of anxiety (1 = lowest level of fear, 2 = second lowest level of fear, and so on). We will begin doing repetitions with the exercises that were rated with the least anxiety (instructions follow).

If your anxiety ratings were never higher than 2, consider the following possible explanations and solutions.

Maybe none of the symptoms of which you are afraid were produced by these exercises. If so, be creative, and come up with other exercises to pro-duce symptoms that are most relevant to you. For example, if you are anx-ious about visual symptoms, look at a bright light for 30 seconds, and then look at a blank wall to see the afterimage. Or, if you are afraid of symp-toms in your throat, put pressure against the sides of your throat, or press down on the back of your tongue with a pen. Another exercise is to sit in a hot, stuffy room for five minutes. You should know by now which symptoms bother you most, so be creative, and invent some ways to produce them. The goal is to deliberately bring on the symptoms that worry you most, as long as it is safe to do. Add these to the "other" category on the Symptom Assessment form, and try them out.

Maybe you stopped the exercises too soon in anticipation of strong symptoms. For example, you might have stopped spinning after 10 seconds because you were just starting to feel off-balance. If so, then repeat the exercises, and try to go for longer.

Maybe you have truly overcome your anxiety of the symptoms as a result of the work you have done so far. If so, we still recommend that you continue with the exercises described below. Overlearning is helpful in the long run.

Maybe you feel so safe in the setting in which you performed the exercise that the symptoms did not scare you. If so, try the exercises when alone or in a place where you feel less safe. Some of our patients note that if they had to do the symptom exercises alone, they would be more frightened. When accompanied, they feel safe, because there is help should something go wrong. Note that this fear is based on a mistaken belief that they would indeed be in danger if the symptoms occurred when they were alone. In fact, these exercises are no more dangerous when alone than when accompanied.

Maybe the knowledge of where the symptoms came from (i.e., the exercise) and the knowledge that the symptoms will go away when the exercise ends decreased your anxiety. Note that this, too, is based on the mistaken notion that unexplained symptoms are necessarily harmful. In this case, continue with the practices, as they should help you manage your fear of symptoms that do arise for no apparent reason.

Repeated Practice With Physical Symptoms

The goals of the repeated practice are to learn something new, including:

- the physical symptoms and anxiety itself are not harmful;

- you can handle the symptoms and the anxiety.

As a result, eventually (although not necessarily immediately), the anxiety about the symptoms will diminish.

You will practice with the exercises that you rated as having at least some similarity (at least a 2 on the similarity rating). Of those, begin with the exercise that you rated with the least anxiety on the 0–10-point scale, as long as the anxiety rating is at least 3. (Do not bother practicing ones with an anxiety rating of 2 or less.)

If you are using benzodiazepine medications (such as Xanax or Klonopin) on an as-needed basis, the temptation may be to take a pill just before you begin to face your fear of the physical symptoms. This is certainly permissible, especially if the only way you are willing to do the symptom exercises is with the help of the medication. However, it will be essential to eventually face your fear and the symptoms without taking the medication (which is described in chapter 11).

Remember, the goal of these exercises is not only to face the symptoms but also the fear and anxiety initially produced by the symptoms, so that you can learn that you can handle the symptoms, fear, and anxiety. Medications, especially short-acting potent benzodiazepines, may actually prevent you from experiencing much fear and anxiety, and in that regard, they become a form of avoidance.

Here are the rules for the repeated practice with physical symptoms.

1. Decide what it is that you are most worried about happening as you practice the symptom exercise, and record that next to the Negative Thoughts header on the Facing Symptoms form on page 162. This may be a concrete outcome, such as fainting, or it may be the idea that you will not be able to handle the anxiety. You may photocopy this form from the book or download multiple copies at the Treatments *ThatWork*™ website (www.oup.com/us/ttw).

2. Begin the exercise, and continue the exercise for at least 30 seconds after the point at which you first notice symptoms. By continuing beyond the point of first noticing the symptoms, you are providing yourself with the chance to learn that the symptoms and anxiety are not harmful—just unpleasant—and that you can handle them.

3. Produce the symptoms as strongly as you can. Do not avoid the symptoms by doing the exercise mildly or with hesitation. For ex-

ample, while spinning, the turning must be continuous, and when overbreathing, make sure that the air is forced out with a lot of pressure and that the breathing rate is fast.

4. Remain focused on what you are doing and feeling in a matter-of-fact way. You will use your coping skills of breathing and thinking *after* each exercise is ended—not during the exercise—because there is not enough time, and it is more important to focus directly on the physical symptoms.

5. When the time is up, stop the exercise, and then complete the Facing Symptoms form to rate:
   - whether the outcome you were most worried about occurred;
   - your level of anxiety (0–10) under the section labeled First Exercise.

6. Now is time to use your coping skills. So, when you finish the exercise, take up to 10 slow, diaphragmatic breaths, and then move into your thinking skills by answering the following questions.
   - What is it that I am most worried about happening?
   - What are the real chances of that happening?
   - What will I do to cope with these symptoms and anxiety?

   Be aware of negative thoughts, such as "I have to stop—I can't handle these feelings." That is a prediction that you are making which is based on nothing but fear. You *can,* in fact, handle the symptoms and continue the exercises. If you have thoughts about the symptoms becoming more intense or lasting longer, or about how they might affect the rest of your day, go back to looking at the real odds, facing the worst, and ways of coping.

7. Wait until your symptoms have abated, and then repeat steps 1–6 two more times.

At the end of each repetition, complete the section on your Facing Symptoms form for the second exercise and then for the third exercise.

Remember to keep in the mind the goal of these exercises. By facing the symptoms and anxiety, you are learning that the symptoms and anxiety are harmless and that you can handle them. As a result, eventually your anxiety over the symptoms will decrease, and eventually, the symptoms will occur less often in your day-to-day life. (Although there will always be some symptoms—remember, everyone has symptoms some of the time.)

Facing Symptoms

Date: _____

Symptom exercise: _____

_____

_____

_____

_____

_____

Negative thought (i.e., whatever it is you are most worried about happening): _____

_____

_____

_____

_____

First Exercise

Did what I most worried about occur? (Yes/No) _____

Maximal anxiety (0–10): _____

Second Exercise

Did what I most worried about occur? (Yes/No) _____

Maximal anxiety (0–10): _____

Third Exercise

Did what I most worried about occur? (Yes/No) _____

Maximal anxiety (0–10): _____

```
         0-------1-------2-------3-------4-------5-------6-------7-------8-------9-------10
            None            Mild         Moderate        Strong         Extreme
```

Do not anxiously wait for the symptoms to abate—that will only fuel your anxiety. Use your thinking skills to help you realize that it does not matter how long the symptoms last, because they are not harmful, and they are tolerable. Anxiously waiting for the symptoms to subside means that you are still worrying about the symptoms. Use the symptom exercises to learn that what you are most worried about in relation to the symptoms does not happen.

Practice the first symptom exercise three times each day over the next week. Continue daily practices of the symptom exercise until your anxiety rating on a given day is no more than 2. That is, it is not so important whether your level of anxiety decreases with each repetition on a given day but whether your anxiety level decreases over each day of practice.

Homework

✎ Continue recording your panic attacks and daily mood using the Panic Attack Record and Daily Mood Record. At the end of the week, add the number of panic attacks and average daily anxiety to your Progress Record.

✎ Practice Changing Your Odds and/or Changing Your Perspective for any panic attacks that occur over this next week.

✎ Practice the Facing the Symptom exercise for your first symptom three times each day, continuing until the maximum anxiety on a given day is no more than 2.

✎ Continue on to section 2 after one week of practice facing symptoms.

Self-Assessment

Answer each of the following by circling T (True) or F (False). Answers are given in the appendix.

1. You should bring on the symptoms to the fullest to get the most benefit out of the symptom exercises.   T   F

2. Stop the symptom exercises as soon as you feel anxious.   T   F

3. The point of the symptom exercises is to learn that the symptoms are not harmful and that the symptoms and anxiety can be handled.   T   F

4. It is best to minimize anxiety by concentrating on slow diaphragmatic breathing and thinking skills as you practice each symptom exercise.   T   F

5. Facing the symptoms will only make you more afraid.   T   F

SECTION 2   *Review of Practice and Continued Practice in Facing Symptoms*

Review of Facing Symptoms

Your task for last week was to practice facing your fear of symptoms every day. By bringing on the symptoms, did you learn that whatever you were most worried about either did not happen or was something you could cope with and that you could handle the symptoms and the anxiety?

Remember to produce the symptoms fully. Also, remember not to distract yourself while you are bringing on the symptoms. An example of distraction would be to think about other things, such as how to manage a difficult situation at home or what to eat for dinner. It is much more helpful to keep a very matter-of-fact attitude in which you are fully focused on what you are doing and on the symptoms that you are producing.

Distraction is similar to avoidance, and avoidance is to be prevented. The best way to learn to be less afraid of symptoms is to face them directly. Usually, avoidance happens because of the continued mistaken belief that the symptoms are harmful (e.g., "I don't want to hyperventilate because I'm afraid that I will pass out and that no one will be there to help me"). Remember, the symptoms are not harmful.

Examples of indirect avoidance include keeping the symptoms at a very mild intensity by doing the exercises only slightly (e.g., breathing only slightly faster than normal during hyperventilation, or spinning at a very slow pace). Or maybe you practiced the symptom exercises only in the presence of someone with whom you feel safe, at times when you felt relaxed, or with the aid of benzodiazepine medications. Either way, these actions represent avoidance. In the end, it will be essential for you to face the symptoms and the anxiety directly, even at very intense levels, or when alone, or at times when already feeling anxious, or without the influence of benzodiazepines, because these are the conditions in which symptoms happen in normal day-to-day life, now or in the future.

Continue to Face Symptoms

From your Symptom Assessment list, progress to the starred (*) exercise that you rated with the next-highest level of anxiety. Practice facing that symptom, remembering the following rules.

1. After you have identified what it is that you are most worried about with the particular symptom exercise (whether that be something concrete, such as fainting, or the idea of not being able to handle the anxiety), begin the exercise.

2. Continue the exercise for at least 30 seconds after the point at which you first notice symptoms. By continuing beyond the point of first noticing the symptoms, you are providing yourself with a chance to learn that the symptoms are not harmful—just unpleasant.

3. Produce the symptoms as strongly as you can. Do not avoid the symptoms by doing the exercise mildly or with hesitation.

4. Remain focused on what you are doing and feeling in a matter-of-fact way. You will use your coping skills of breathing and thinking *after* each exercise is ended—not during the exercise.

5. When the time is up, stop the exercise, and then rate:
   - whether the outcome you were most worried about occurred;
   - your level of anxiety (0–10) under the section labeled First Exercise.

6. Now is the time to use your coping skills. So, when you finish the exercise, take up to 10 slow, diaphragmatic breaths, and then move into calm thinking by answering the following questions.
   - What is it that I am most worried about happening?
   - What are the real chances of that happening?
   - What will I do to cope with these symptoms?

7. Wait until your symptoms have abated, and then repeat steps 1–6 two more times.

At the end of each repetition, complete the section on your Facing Symptoms form for the second exercise and then for the third exercise.

Continue in this way until you have practiced each starred (*) symptom exercise three times a day and for enough days so that the maximum anxiety rating on a given day is no higher than 2.

Homework

✎ Continue recording your panic attacks and daily mood using the Panic Attack Record and Daily Mood Record. At the end of the week, add your number of panic attacks and daily average anxiety to your Progress Record.

✎ Practice Changing Your Odds and/or Changing Your Perspective for any panic attacks that occur over this next week.

✎ Practice facing the starred symptom exercises three times each day for the number of days necessary for your anxiety rating on a given day to be no more than 2. Continue in this way until you have sufficiently practiced each starred symptom exercise.

✎ Move to section 3 when you have completed at least one half of your starred symptom exercises.

Self-Assessment

Answer each of the following by circling T (True) or F (False). Answers are given in the appendix.

1. As you face the physical symptoms, keep your mind preoccupied with other things.   T   F

2. Stop the symptom exercises when your maximum anxiety is no higher than 5.   T   F

3. The purpose of facing the symptoms is to become less anxious about the symptoms, but it is not to eliminate the symptoms.   T   F

SECTION 3 *Facing Symptoms in Activities*

Facing the Fear Out There: Activities

Up until now, your efforts have been directed at artificial exercises, such as hyperventilation and spinning—activities that are not common in day-to-day life. Now, it is time to move to more common activities that you have feared or avoided because of the physical symptoms they cause. Examples include: drinking coffee (because of the stimulant effect), eating chocolate (because of the stimulant effect), aerobic activity (because of the cardio-vascular effect), lifting heavy objects (because of the heightened blood pressure and dizziness effects), and so on. A more comprehensive list is provided below in the Activities Hierarchy. As you look through the items on this list, you may realize that you have been avoiding these types of activities, and only now is the reason clear—because these activities bring on bodily symptoms that remind you of panic attacks.

Rate each activity from 0 to 10, where 0 = no anxiety at all and 10 = extreme anxiety. Any activities that you rated as 3 or above will now be part of your Activities Hierarchy, and, as with the symptom exercises up until now, the goal is to repeat each activity as many times as needed to learn that the symptoms are not dangerous (i.e., that whatever you are most worried about never happens or rarely happens and that you can cope with whatever happens) and that the symptoms and anxiety can be handled. You will know this when the next time you practice a given activity, the maximum anxiety level is 2 or less.

This takes a lot of work, because these activities often take more time than the symptom exercises. However, the more you put into it, the more you will improve.

Also, there is a difference between the symptom exercises and some of the activities that you are just beginning. With the symptom exercises, the symp-

Activities Hierarchy

Activity	Anxiety (0–10)
Running up flights of stairs	_____
Walking outside in intense heat	_____
Attending meetings in hot, stuffy rooms	_____
Driving in hot, stuffy cars	_____
Shopping in hot, stuffy stores or shopping malls	_____
Walking outside in very cold weather	_____
Participating in aerobics	_____
Lifting heavy objects	_____
Dancing	_____
Engaging in sexual relations	_____
Watching horror movies	_____
Eating heavy meals	_____
Watching exciting movies or sporting events	_____
Getting involved in "heated" debates	_____
Showering with the doors and windows closed	_____
Using a sauna	_____
Hiking	_____
Playing sports	_____
Drinking coffee or other caffeinated beverages	_____
Eating chocolate	_____
Standing quickly from a sitting position	_____
Getting angry	_____
Riding fairground or amusement park rides	_____
Snorkeling	_____
Taking antihistamines or other over-the-counter medications	_____
Looking up at the sky and clouds	_____
Drinking diet cola and other sodas	_____
Reading while a passenger in a car	_____
For persons who frequently panic out of sleep:	
Deep meditative relaxation	_____
Fatigue from staying up late several nights in a row	_____
Alcohol or antihistamines	_____
Abrupt wakening from sleep by an alarm that goes off in the middle of the night	_____
Hot sleeping conditions due to central heating, windows closed, no air conditioning or fans, on warm nights, or from wearing warm clothes to bed	_____

toms generally build up quickly after starting the exercise and subside quickly after you stop the exercise. This not always true with the activities. For example, symptoms may not come on right away after drinking coffee because it takes time for caffeine to have its peak effect (about 45 minutes). Similarly, the symptoms may not go away immediately after drinking coffee. The important point to keep in mind is that even though you do not know exactly when symptoms will come and go, the symptoms are not harmful.

Facing Your Own Activities

Choose the activity that you rated about 3 in terms of anxiety, and then follow the steps below.

1. Identify what it is that you are most worried about happening in this activity. This is called *Negative Thought*. As with the Facing Symptom exercises, this might be a concrete outcome, such as dying or fainting, or it might be the idea that you cannot handle the anxiety associated with the activity.

2. Think about the best conditions in which to practice, so that you can truly learn that your negative thoughts are unrealistic (these are called *End Goals*). For example, let us say that your task is to have a shower with the windows and doors closed, so that the room fills up with steam. In the past, you may have avoided doing this because the steam led you to feel a sense of suffocation. So, the plan might be to close the doors and windows before you turn on the water, run the hot water for a few minutes before you get into the shower, and then stay in the shower for a particular period of time, such as 10 minutes, even if you feel a sense of suffocation. (Remember, a sense of suffocation does not mean that you are actually suffocating.) Then, get out of the shower, and dry off in the steamy room for a couple of minutes before opening the door. Another example is deciding to overcome your fear of hot, stuffy areas. In the past, you have avoided wearing heavy clothes, especially in crowded places such as shopping malls. So, your goal is to wear a coat or a thick sweater in an already warm mall.

Facing Activities (1)

Date: _____

Activity: _Jogging._ _____

End Goals (excluding superstitious objects, safety signals, safety behaviors, and distractions): _Jog 20 minutes alone._

Today's Goals: _Jog five minutes with running group._ _____

Negative Thought (i.e., whatever it is you are most worried about happening): _I will become breathless and stop_

breathing. _____

Figure 10.2.

Example of Part of Completed Facing Activities Form (1)

As with facing agoraphobia situations, learning that your negative thoughts are unrealistic will require that you let go of all superstitious objects, safety signals, safety behaviors, or distractions. So, go back to your lists of Superstitious/Safety Signals and Safety Behaviors/Distractions from chapter 4, and plan for eventually practicing each activity without anything on those lists.

3. Choose either gradually to work up to the End Goals of the activity or to go directly to the End Goals of the activity. For example, let us say that your plan is to drink a cup of coffee, and you decide to take a gradual rather than a direct approach. Therefore, your first step is to drink a full cup of decaffeinated coffee, since usually you avoid even the small amount of caffeine in decaffeinated brews. The next step is to drink a mixture of decaffeinated and caffeinated coffee. Finally, you drink a full cup of caffeinated coffee. Or, if you wanted to take a direct approach, you could just go straight to drinking a full cup of caffeinated coffee. Today's Goals are the conditions in which you will practice on a given day as you work toward your End Goals.

In preparation for the practice, ask yourself the following questions.

■ Has what you are most worried about ever happened? (If it has not happened or rarely has, then you are jumping to conclusions.)

■ What is the worst that can happen, and how would you cope with it? (If the worst feels unbearable and you feel as if you could not cope, then you are blowing things out of proportion.)

Facing Activities (2)

Negative Thought: _I will become breathless and stop breathing._

How many times has it happened? _None._

What is the evidence? _Even though I feel breathless, I am healthy and unlikely to stop breathing._

What are the real odds? (0–100): _Zero._

Ways of coping: _I will go slowly and remind myself that breathlessness is not dangerous._

Figure 10.3.

Example of Part of Completed Facing Activities Form (2)

Then:
a. look at all the evidence;
b. consider the real odds;
c. realize that the worst is probably not as bad as you first thought; and
d. think of ways of coping.

This activity is to be practiced at least three times over the next week (either going straight to your End Goals or gradually working up to your End Goals across each practice). If your situation is very brief (e.g., looking up at the clouds moving across the sky), then continue practicing over and over again on a given day until you spend about one hour practicing.

You will continue to practice a given activity the number of days necessary for your maximum anxiety level to reduce to 2 or less. Whether your level of anxiety decreases or not within a given practice is not important; what is more important is that over each day of practice, the level of anxiety eventually decreases. Now, we will consider ways of making the practice as effective as possible.

Moment of Fear

If you become afraid or nervous during the activity, manage your anxiety so that you can continue the activity by first using your breathing skills.

- Focus your attention on breathing and counting.

- Count for one second, inhale for two seconds, think the word "relax" for one second, and exhale for two seconds.

- Expand your stomach when you breathe in, and deflate your stomach when you breathe out, keeping your chest relatively still, without taking big breaths.

- Count up to 10 and back to 1, one time.

Then, ask yourself the following key questions so that you can begin your thinking skills.

- What is it that I am most worried about happening?

- What are the real chances of that happening?

- What will I do to cope with and manage this situation?

Remember, the goal of the breathing and thinking skills is not to eliminate the symptoms or the anxiety but to help you to continue moving forward in facing your fears and completing the activity.

Incomplete Practice

If, while you are doing your activity, you feel as if you absolutely have to leave because your fear and anxiety are so intense, the best strategy is to leave the activity *temporarily* and, after you have used your coping skills, return to the activity again. So, for example, if you are in an aerobics class, you may leave the class in order to practice breathing, ask yourself the same key questions listed above to help you to use your thinking skills, and then return to the class. Or, if you are dancing, hiking, or looking up at the sky and clouds, you may take a break, use your breathing and thinking skills, and then return to the activity. (Of course, there will be some activities from which it will be impossible to temporarily leave.)

The number-one rule is that if you escape from an activity and do not return to it, you will end up back where you started and not make progress. So you must always return to the activity.

After the Practice

After the practice is completed:

- rate whether what you were most worried about occurred or not (yes or no);

Facing Activities

Date: _____

Activity: _____

_____

_____

End Goals (excluding superstitious objects, safety signals, safety behaviors, and distractions): _____

_____

_____

Today's Goals: _____

_____

_____

Negative Thought (i.e., whatever it is you are most worried about happening): _____

_____

_____

How many times has it happened? _____

What is the evidence? _____

_____

What are the real odds? (0–100) _____

Ways of coping: _____

_____

_____

_____

Did what I most worried about occur? (Yes/No) _____

Maximal anxiety (0–10): _____

```
0 ------ 1 ------ 2 ------ 3 ------ 4 ------ 5 ------ 6 ------ 7 ------ 8 ------ 9 ------ 10
    None         Mild         Moderate         Strong         Extreme
```

- rate your level of maximal anxiety during the practice on a 0–10-point scale, where 0 = no anxiety and 10 = extreme anxiety.

You may photocopy this form from the book or download multiple copies at the Treatments *ThatWork*™ website (www.oup.com/us/ttw).

Jill's activities for her first two weeks were to attend a fitness class (10 minutes each time, first with a friend and then alone) and to have a shower with the curtain drawn and the door closed. The first time she attended a fitness class, she was very anxious before the class but practiced slow breathing and reminded herself that although she may feel out of breath, hot, sweaty, and a suffering from a pounding heart, she was not in danger. As soon as the class started, Jill wanted to leave, but then she realized that by going at her own pace, she could handle the feelings, and so she stayed for the full 10 minutes. After the first practice, it became easier, and Jill stayed for longer periods in the class. Then she went to class alone. Her fears in the shower were related to negative thoughts about suffocating from a lack of air. She gradually increased the length of time in the steamy shower room.

Medication Issues

As with the symptom exercises, the use of medication has to be considered: particularly, medications that either block all of your feelings or that you rely on to reduce your fear at the moment. (The latter are the fast-acting medications, such as Xanax and Klonopin.)

If medications are so potent that they block all feelings, then they may interfere with the benefits that you can receive from facing your fear. That is, some anxiety is very helpful—we learn more when we are anxious in comparison to when we are completely relaxed. Also, it is important to learn that physical symptoms and fear and anxiety are not harmful. So, if your anxiety and panic are completely blocked by medications, it may be helpful to talk with your prescriber about lowering the dosage of your medication.

The second issue concerns the use of fast-acting medications. Initially, when you first face activities that bring on bodily symptoms, you may feel the need for Xanax or Klonopin, because those medications have been your usual coping tool. That is okay, as long as you eventually become comfortable enough so that you can do these activities without the fast-acting medications. That way, you will really get the chance to learn that the bodily symptoms produced by the activity are not harmful. Ways of weaning off medications are described in chapter 11.

General Issues

Some of the activities will take special planning, and it may take some time to accomplish all of the activities on your list. However, it is important to practice regularly—do not put it off!

Given the timing issues, it sometimes makes sense to work on two activities at one time. For example, you could exercise every second or third day, building up your fitness level, while at the same time practice getting used to steamy showers once or twice a day.

Homework

✎ Continue recording your panic attacks and daily mood using the Panic Attack Record and Daily Mood Record. At the end of the week, add the number of panic attacks and daily average anxiety to your Progress Record.

✎ Practice either Changing Your Odds and/or Changing Your Perspective for any panic attacks that occur over this next week.

✎ Practice your first activity at least three days a week, and continue to do so until your anxiety rating on a given day is no more than 2. You may work on more than one activity at a time.

✎ Continue to section 4 once you have completed at least one week of practice with an activity.

Self-Assessment

Answer each of the following by circling T (True) or F (False). Answers are given in the appendix.

1. I should avoid caffeine and any other stimulants.   T   F

2. It is dangerous to make myself feel unpleasant physical feelings by sitting in a sauna or by weight training.   T   F

3. If I become anxious as I face an activity, I should stop and try a different activity.   T   F

4. I should always complete the activity to its fullest degree and never proceed gradually.   T   F

5. I should continue the activity with the aid of breathing and thinking skills, even if I experience symptoms.   T   F

SECTION 4   *Review and Planning for Continued Facing Activities*

Reminder of the Value of Facing Activities

As a reminder, the purpose of the activity practices is for you to learn that the symptoms that are produced by these activities are not harmful, that you can handle the symptoms and the anxiety, and that you can accomplish something you have been avoiding. Consequently, your anxiety over the activities will eventually decrease.

Review of Practicing Facing Activities

Did you practice an activity at least three days last week? If you have not practiced regularly, we encourage you to make these practices a priority. It takes effort, but the more effort you expend, the more benefit that you will gain. Remember to keep records of your practices on your Facing Activities form, so that you can learn that the symptoms produced by the activity are not harmful and that you can handle the symptoms and the anxiety. Eventually, with repetition, your anxiety will decrease.

Did you try one of your activities, become frightened, and escape? For example, did you sit in a sauna and leave as soon as you felt too hot, or did you stop drinking from your cup of coffee after the first sip or two? If so, then spend some time thinking about why. What led to your escape? What kind of symptoms did you feel? What kind of negative thoughts were going through your mind? What catastrophe were you anticipating had you continued with the activity? After identifying the mistaken negative thought, look at the evidence, and put things back into perspective. Then, repeat the activity so that you can confirm that the symptoms it causes are harmless. Let us say that you left an aerobics class before the designated time. After some thought, you realize that you left because you thought your heart rate was far too fast, that it was reaching a dangerously high speed, and that you might pass out or collapse. Then you looked at the evidence and realized that heart rates are supposed to go fast when people exercise; that it probably was not going as fast as you thought; and that even if it was going very fast, the chances of passing out or collapsing were very slim. After that kind of analysis, you felt more able to go back and complete the aerobics class.

Remember that these practices are not supposed to be associated with zero anxiety or fear. That is, you should feel afraid at first, or else there would be no need to do them at all. Furthermore, sometimes the fear increases at first before it decreases, because you are facing things that scare you. However, with repeated practice, the anxiety will eventually decrease.

Continued Facing Activities

Continue to practice with each activity that you rated with an anxiety level of 3 or higher in section 1, using the steps outlined in section 1.

Homework

✎ Continue recording your panic attacks and daily mood using the Panic Attack Record and Daily Mood Record. At the end of the week, add the number of panic attacks and daily average anxiety to your Progress Record.

✎ Practice either Changing Your Odds and/or Changing Your Perspective for any panic attacks that occur over this next week.

✎ Practice each activity at least three days a week, and continue to do so until your anxiety rating on a given day is no more than 2. You may work on more than one activity at a time.

Answer each of the following by circling T (True) or F (False). Answers are given in the appendix.

1. I should practice each activity the number of times necessary for me to learn that the symptoms are not harmful and that I can handle the symptoms and the anxiety.   T   F

2. If the symptoms continue for a long time after an activity such as drinking coffee, that does not mean that the symptoms are dangerous. Instead, it means that I am probably preoccupied with the symptoms.   T   F

3. It is not terribly important for me to record what I was worried about happening on my Facing Activities form as long as I complete the activities.   T   F

4. The activities should be discontinued if they create too much anxiety or too many symptoms.   T   F

Chapter 11   *Medications*

Goals

- To learn about medications for anxiety and panic

- To learn ways in which medications can be used in combination with the methods outlined in this program

- To learn ways of weaning yourself off medications

SECTION 1   *Medications for Anxiety*

Many people with anxiety and panic attacks have had doctors prescribe medications. If this is true for you, you may take this medication regularly or perhaps only when you feel you need it. Many people go through this program without ever starting medication; others would just as soon not take the medication but are doing so on the advice of their physicians. However, there are a number of people who want medication for their anxiety and/or panic attacks. For some, the anxiety and panic are so severe that they feel they cannot handle even one more day and need relief as soon as possible. Even the medication that takes the longest to act would begin to take effect in three weeks. Some of the shorter-acting medications can work within a day or two. Others may not feel that they have the time to devote to mastering the information in this workbook right now. Still others may believe strongly that medication is the best treatment for their anxiety.

In any case, almost 60% of the people who come to our clinic for psychological treatment are taking some kind of medication for their anxiety. Some have been taking it for quite some time. For others, their physician has given them a prescription to get them through a few weeks but has told them to come to our clinic as soon as possible.

As we mentioned in chapter 1, we do not recommend that these people stop taking their medications before starting the program. Eventually, many people stop taking medication on their own. About one half of the people stop taking medications by the time they finish this program, and others stop sometime during the first year after finishing. Below, we describe ways to stop taking medications if you want to do so.

At this point, the evidence seems clear that some types of medications, if prescribed at the right dosage, can be effective for at least the short-term relief of anxiety or panic for some people. Many of these medications, however, are not effective in the long term unless you continue to take them. Even then, they may lose some of their effectiveness unless you learn some new, more helpful methods of coping with your anxiety and panic while you are on the medication. Nevertheless, there are some people who begin a course of medication therapy and stop several months later without any need to go through a program such as this. Whether the particular stress they were under has resolved, whether there were some changes in their sensitivity, or whether they developed a different attitude toward their anxiety and panic, medication for this short time was all they needed.

For all of these reasons, it seems useful to review the ways in which medications work and the different types of medications prescribed for anxiety and panic.

How Do Medications Work?

Medications are believed to decrease vulnerability to experiencing panic and anxiety. Medications seem to make it harder for the body to have a full fear reaction. In addition, medications reduce general anxiety and, therefore, reduce the severity of daily worry about panic attacks. Because the symptoms of general anxiety are reduced, there are fewer symptoms to become afraid of in a "fear of fear" cycle.

Medications decrease panic and anxiety by changing the proportions of neurotransmitters (i.e., chemicals) in certain parts of your brain and nervous system. This process of adjustment in the brain chemistry often takes several weeks, which is why many medications do not work immediately (although some do). During this adjustment, the brain "rebalances" itself. Therefore, medication is not giving your brain something extra that it lacks, nor is it taking away something that the brain has too much of. Rather, it is helping your brain rebalance and work more efficiently doing the job it has to do.

Imagine that the brain has a stress "thermostat" that keeps it in balance, like a thermostat keeps a room the same temperature when the temperature gets too hot or too cold. Panic and anxiety may occur when the "set point" that determines the ideal level (i.e., temperature) gets moved too high or too low. For example, stress can move the set point. So can certain substances, such as caffeine. The process of rebalancing moves the set point back to the middle so that the brain can work more like it has before. After some time, medication may no longer be needed, provided that you can develop better ways of coping with stress so that future stressful events do not move the thermostat set point out of balance again.

Different Types of Medications

Antidepressants

There are several classes of antidepressants which control anxiety and panic attacks. Antidepressants called serotonin-specific reuptake inhibitors (SSRIs) include medications such as fluoxetine (Prozac), sertraline (Zoloft), fluvoxamine (Luvox), and paroxetine (Paxil). Related antidepressants called serotonin-norepinepherine reuptake inhibitors (SNRIs) include venlafaxine (Effexor) and serzone (Nefazodone). These two classes of medications have become first-line drug treatments for panic disorder. In general, they are less toxic and cause fewer side effects than older medications such as tricyclic antidepressants and monamine oxidase inhibitors (described next). Nevertheless, some people still experience stomach upset and other gastrointestinal symptoms, headaches, and other side effects—particularly, sexual dysfunction—with these medications. In addition, there may be some initial worsening of anxiety, although this can be decreased by starting with lower doses (such as 5 mg of Prozac). The most effective doses for controlling panic and anxiety for drugs most often prescribed are 20–40 mg of Prozac, 75–150 mg of Luvox, 20–40 mg of Paxil, and 100–200 mg of Zoloft (see Table 11.1).

Tricyclic antidepressants include imipramine (Tofranil), clomipramine (Anafranil), desipramine (Norpramin), nortriptyline (Pamelor), and amitriptyline (Elavil). Tofranil was formerly the most commonly used antidepressant for anxiety and panic but has been largely supplanted by SSRIs, as noted above. These medications are generally helpful for panic and anxiety when administered in the range of 150–300 mg of Tofranil or its equivalent. There may be some worsening of anxiety initially. However, the initial worsening is only small when beginning with small doses (such as 10 mg of Tofranil). These doses are gradually increased to effective levels. Also, the initial worsening goes away after the first week or so of treatment. Other side effects include dry mouth, constipation, blurred vision, weight gain, and lightheadedness. However, these side effects are generally harmless and go away after a few weeks. It usually takes several weeks before the medications control anxiety and panic. So, getting through the first few weeks is critical. It is difficult because the first few weeks are when the side effects are the strongest, but the medication is not yet having a positive effect on reducing panic and anxiety. After that, the side effects decrease, and so do panic and anxiety.

Another type of antidepressant medication is the monoamine-oxidase (MAO) inhibitors. The best-known medication in this category for anxiety and panic is phenelzine (Nardil). Others include tranylcypromine (Parnate) and isocarboxazid (Marplan). MAO inhibitors can cause side effects such as lightheadedness, weight gain, muscle twitching, sexual dysfunction, and sleep disturbance. As with other medications, treatment usually begins with low doses, such as 15–30 mg per day of Nardil, and is gradually increased to effective levels, such as 60–90 mg per day of Nardil. The MAO inhibitors are seldom used for panic disorder these days because there are severe dietary restrictions when on this medication. For example, you cannot eat cheese, chocolate, or other foods containing tyramine, and you cannot drink red wine or beer. If you do, you risk dangerous symptoms, including high blood pressure.

The antidepressant medications seem to be about equally effective for panic attacks, anxiety, and agoraphobia. One thorny problem with antidepressant medications is the side effects during the first few weeks. In addition, the side effects are sometimes similar to symptoms of panic and anxiety. For that reason, many people do not want to continue taking the antidepressant or at least do not want to increase the dosage to the levels that are needed to reduce panic and anxiety (this is called the *therapeutic dosage*). And yet, research has shown that it is important to take enough of this medication to get the full benefits. Therefore, it is best to stick it out through the first few weeks until reaching the therapeutic dosage. To help you stick it out, remember the following.

1. Side effects are not an indication of something wrong or harmful happening to your body. That is, the side effects do not indicate that physical damage is occurring to your body. Nor do they indicate a physical disease. In fact, side effects indicate that medications are having their intended chemical effects.

2. Side effects are not an indication that your anxiety is increasing. Instead, side effects indicate that your body is going through a period of adjustment to the medication, and sometimes, the side effects of this adjustment are symptoms that are similar to panic anxiety—but they are not actual panic and anxiety.

3. Side effects usually go away after a few weeks.

4. Strategies described in this treatment will help you to be less afraid of the side effects and achieve therapeutic dosages of medication.

It is much easier to stop taking antidepressants than benzodiazepines (described below). In other words, there are usually fewer withdrawal symptoms when antidepressants are ended than when benzodiazepines are ended. Therefore, the relapse rates are much lower for antidepressants (around 40–50%) than for benzodiazepines.

Benzodiazepines

Medications commonly prescribed for anxiety and panic in the past, but less frequently now, are the minor tranquilizers. Two of the most common are diazepam (Valium) and chlordiazepoxide (Librium). Typically, these medications are prescribed for short-term relief of anxiety. They are generally believed to be unhelpful for panic attacks unless they are prescribed in very high dosages. For example, you might need 30 mg or more of Valium per day to make a dent in your panic attacks. At this dosage, chances are that you would feel very sedated (i.e., sleepy). For this reason, minor tranquilizers are not usually prescribed for panic attacks by psychiatrists and physicians knowledgeable in the medication treatment of panic. Also, over time, you may need increasingly larger dosages of the medication to obtain the same effects. This is called *tolerance*. Unless you work carefully with your physician, there is a danger that with long-term usage, you may become psychologically and physically dependent on medication (i.e., suffer addiction) that had been intended only for short-term treatment of anxiety.

High-potency medications have stronger effects per dose than lower-potency medications. High-potency benzodiazepines alleviate panic attacks without causing such side effects as extreme sleepiness, which are seen with higher doses of lower-potency benzodiazepines (e.g., Valium). These medications work very quickly; their effects are usually noticeable within 20 minutes of ingestion and are still the most frequently prescribed medications for panic and anxiety. The best-known high-potency benzodiazepines are alprazolam (Xanax) and clonazepam (Klonopin). To give you an idea of how strong Xanax is, 1 mg of Xanax equals approximately 10 mg of Valium. The therapeutic dose of Xanax for panic attacks varies from person to person and also with the nature of the panic attacks. Usually, 1–4 mg per day would be the best dosage for panic attacks, but a dosage of more than 4 mg per day is sometimes required for severe agoraphobia avoidance. With these doses, 60% of a large group of patients were free of panic after eight weeks. The appropriate dose of Klonopin is 1.5–4 mg per day.

Side effects of these medications include sleepiness, poor coordination, and memory problems. However, starting with low doses and gradually increasing over time can reduce these side effects. The initial feeling of sleepiness usually subsides as one adapts to the medication. It is important to realize that the side effects decrease over time and are not dangerous.

The different benzodiazepines differ in how long they remain active in your body. This is referred to as *half-life* (or, the amount of time it takes for one half of a dose of medication to be eliminated from the body). With longer half-life, medication is taken less frequently. Klonopin has a longer half-life (15–50 hours) than Xanax (12–15 hours). Therefore, Klonopin is taken less frequently than Xanax. With a medication of shorter half-life, people often feel the effects of the medication wearing off and notice increased anxiety when the levels of medication in the body are low, such as when wake in the morning.

Benzodiazepines are believed to work by increasing the effect of a chemical in the brain called gamma amino butyric acid (GABA). GABA is distributed throughout the brain. It functions to inhibit the firing of nerve cells. Benzodiazepines help GABA to "put the brakes on" those areas of the brain which cause anxiety. As you can probably imagine, stopping benzodiazepines will "let up on the brakes" and is usually associated with an increase in anxiety. This is one reason why many (if not most) people relapse when they stop benzodiazepines.

Withdrawal symptoms are felt when benzodiazepines are stopped. These include anxiety, jitteriness, difficulty concentrating, irritability, sensitivity to light or sound, muscle tension or aching, headaches, sleep disturbance, and stomach upset. Sometimes these withdrawal symptoms lead people to become very concerned and anxious, especially because the withdrawal symptoms are similar to symptoms of panic and anxiety. People are sometimes so upset by the withdrawal symptoms that they begin the medication again in order to get rid of the withdrawal symptoms. Alternatively, they may relapse (i.e., suffer a recurrence of panic and anxiety). Relapse is especially likely if the withdrawal symptoms are mistakenly viewed as being harmful. Actually, most withdrawal symptoms are not harmful. Instead, withdrawal symptoms reflect the body's adjustments to the chemical changes. Also, withdrawal symptoms go away with time. With this type of information and some other behavioral strategies, the withdrawal process is generally much easier. Thus, slow tapering off of benzodiazepines, combined with the types of strategies described in this workbook, dramatically reduces withdrawal and relapse when benzodiazepines are discontinued.

Beta-Blockers

Many people take *beta-blockers* to reduce blood pressure or regulate heart rate. These medications act on a specific receptor, the *beta-receptor,* which is involved in regulating aspects of body functioning such as heart rate. Therefore, if one needs to avoid physical tension for medical reasons, beta-blockers are often used. There are many types of beta-blockers, but the most popular is propranolol (Inderal). Given the information about the psychological factors involved in panic disorder, especially the notion of anxiety focused on physical symptoms of fear, one would think that any medication that decreases bodily symptoms such as fast heart rates would eliminate panic attacks. But there is little if any evidence that Inderal is useful in any way for panic attacks, although some people might feel a little

Table 11.1. Medications Used to Treat Panic Disorder

Medication	Brand Name	Initial Dose	Dosage Range
FDA-Approved Drugs for Panic Disorder			
SSRIs			
Fluoxetine	Prozac	10 mg/day	10–60 mg/day
Paroxetine	Paxil	10 mg/day	10–60 mg/day
Sertraline	Zoloft	25 mg/day	50–200 mg/day
Benzodiazepines			
Alprazolam	Xanax	0.25–0.5 mg/day (3 times per day)	0.25–4 mg/day (3 times per day)
Clonazepam	Klonopin	0.25 mg/day	1–3 mg/day
Not Approved by FDA at This Time for Panic Disorder			
SSRIs			
Escitalopran	Lexapro	10 mg/day	10–50 mg/day
Citalopram	Celexa	10 mg/day	20–60 mg/day
Fluvoxamine	Luvox	25 mg/day	25–300 mg/day
SNRIs			
Venlafaxine	Effexor	37.5 mg/day	73–300 mg/day
Nefazodone Hydrochloride	Serzone	200 mg/day	300–600 mg/day
Benzodiazepines			
Diazepan	Valium	4 mg/day	4–40 mg/day
TCAs			
Imipramine	Tofranil	75 mg/day	50–200 mg/day
Clompramine	Anafranil	25 mg/day	25–250 mg/day

bit better. For that reason, doctors knowledgeable about the medication treatment of anxiety almost never prescribe this as the main medication to treat anxiety and panic. It is sometimes included as an adjunct or secondary medication.

Medications with indications approved by the Food and Drug Administration for panic disorder are listed in Table 11.1, along with additional medications that, although not specifically approved, are likely to be just as effective in certain instances for some people. As always, your physician should work with you in making the final decisions on which medication is best for you.

Now that you have finished this program, you should be ready to stop your medication, if you wish to do so. If this is a particularly difficult problem for you, an additional brief program for stopping medications with proven effectiveness is available from the Treatments *ThatWork*™ series available from Oxford University Press called *Stopping Anxiety Medication*. Be very sure that you stop your medication under the supervision of your physician; only your doctor can decide how quickly it will be safe for you to taper off your medication to the point where you can stop it altogether. This will be particularly true for medications like Xanax, which are best tapered off very slowly. With what you have learned from this program, you should have little trouble stopping your medication if you follow these general guidelines.

1.   Withdraw from your medication relatively slowly. Do not try to do it all at once. Once again, your physician will be able to give you the best advice on how fast is best for you.

2.   Set a target date for stopping your medication. Once again, this will have to be planned with your physician, so make it a reasonable date in view of your own tapering-off schedule. On the other hand, the date should not be too far away. Generally, the quicker, the better— as long as it is within a schedule that is safe for you, as determined by your physician.

3.   Use the principles and coping skills that you have learned in this workbook as you withdraw from the medication.

The reason that we have not addressed this topic until now is because it is important for you to learn how to master your anxiety and panic before successfully stopping medication. One reason for this is that you may begin to experience anxiety and panic at more intense levels as you come off the medication. If you were never on medication, you should have mastered panic and anxiety by now. If you are on medication, the principles you have learned will need to be applied again to deal with some increased anxiety and panic as you come off medication. Once again, most people do not find this a problem and gradually reduce their medication as they become more comfortable in dealing with their anxiety and panic.

If your anxiety and panic seem to be increasing as you decrease your medication dose, it is most likely due to mild withdrawal symptoms. The symptoms simply reflect your body readjusting to the chemical changes of having the medication withdrawn. The withdrawal symptoms do not mean that you must go back on the medication, nor do they mean that something is seriously wrong with you. Instead, the withdrawal symptoms mean a period of adjustment, and they should last only a week or two (in rare cases, a little longer), until the medication clears from your system. In addition, you now have the skills to handle these symptoms. This is a perfect opportunity to use your skills of breathing, relaxing, looking at the evidence, and putting things back into perspective.

In this way, withdrawal from medication can be seen as the last item on your list of activities described in chapter 10. That is, withdrawing from medication is another way to produce physical feelings of which you are, or at least were, afraid. Therefore, medication withdrawal can be added to your list of activities, and it can be treated as an opportunity to practice breathing and looking at the evidence to avoid jumping to conclusions and putting things back into perspective about the withdrawal symptoms. Rather than becoming distressed at the physical feelings that you experience as you withdraw from medications, follow the guidelines in chapter 10 for learning to be less afraid of them.

After you withdraw from medications, it is very important that you face all of the symptoms, activities, and situations that you faced while on the medication.

Homework

✎ If you are on medication and wish to withdraw, then your assignment for this week is to speak with your prescribing physician about the best way to do so.

✎ Plan how you will deal with any of the withdrawal symptoms by using the various skills that you have learned in this program.

✎ Draw up a specific step-by-step plan for yourself.

Answer each of the following by circling true (T) or false (F). Answers can be found in the appendix.

1. It is essential that withdrawal from medication is conducted gradually, under the supervision of your prescribing physician.   T   F

2. You are unlikely to feel any different when you withdraw from your medication.   T   F

3. Use physical symptoms, anxiety, or panic that you experience when withdrawing from medication as an opportunity to breathe slowly from the abdomen, change mistaken beliefs, and face your fear.   T   F

4. Experiencing physical symptoms or anxiety and panic when withdrawing from medication is a sign of a loss of all your treatment gains.   T   F

5. Experiencing physical symptoms or anxiety and panic when withdrawing from medication is a sign that you will not be able to get off the medication.   T   F

6. The great majority of patients who have completed this program are able to get off their medications.   T   F

Chapter 12

Accomplishments, Maintenance, and Relapse Prevention

Goals

■ Evaluate your progress

■ Learn how to structure continued practice

■ Ways of maintaining progress

■ High-risk times and management of setbacks

Evaluate Your Progress

It is time to consider the kind of changes that you have made since you first began this program. This can be done in several ways. Using your Progress Record, compare the frequency of panic attacks from the beginning to this point, and examine the course of change throughout the program. There may indeed be ups and downs. Also, compare the severity of your daily anxiety from the beginning to now. If the frequency of your panic attacks and/or the severity of your anxiety have decreased, check YES next to the item labeled panic and anxiety in the list below. If not, check NO.

Second, look at your thoughts. Have you made significant changes in the ways you think about panic, anxiety, and the physical symptoms? In other words, are you much less likely to jump to conclusions and to blow things out of proportion, particularly when it comes to panic and the physical symptoms of panic? If so, then check the YES box for the item labeled Negative Thoughts. If not, check NO.

Third, look at your initial fear ratings for your hierarchies of symptoms and activities. Now, rate your current level of fear of the same symptoms and activities, using the same 0–10-point scale (where 0 = no fear and 10 = extreme fear). Are you able to handle physical symptoms produced by hyperventilation, spinning, holding your breath, exercising, drinking

Progress Evaluation

Evaluate your own progress since you began this program.

Panic and Anxiety

Significant reduction in frequency of panic, severity of panic, or level of anxiety about panic. ☐ Yes   ☐ No

Negative Thoughts

Significant reduction in jumping to conclusions and blowing things out of proportion. ☐ Yes   ☐ No

Symptom and Activity Exercises

Significant reduction in "fear of symptom induction" exercises and activities. ☐ Yes   ☐ No

Agoraphobia Situations

Significant reduction in fear and/or avoidance of situations associated with panic. ☐ Yes   ☐ No

coffee, or watching a horror movie with much less fear than the first time you rated these various exercises? If there has been a significant reduction in your fear of these items, check YES next to the item labeled Symptoms and Activities. If not, check NO.

Fourth, look at your initial fear ratings for your Hierarchy of Agoraphobia Situations. Now, rate your current level of fear of the same situations using the 0–10-point scale (where 0 = no fear and 10 = extreme fear). Are you able to consider driving, flying, being alone, being away from home, and so on with much less fear than when you first rated these situations? If so, check YES next to the item labeled Situations. If not, check NO.

If you have checked the YES box for at least three of the four items, you may consider that you have done very well with this program. If, on the other hand, you have checked NO to three or more items, there is still room for gains to be made.

What to Do Next

You may have a number of activities or situations to practice. Use the Practice Plan on page 194 to list all of the things to be practiced over the next few weeks in terms of:

Practice Plan

Things to Practice	Description
Breathing Skills	*More practice returning fast, shallow breathing back to a slow and abdominal pattern; go back to practice of 10 minutes, twice per day, in relaxing places.*
Thinking Skills	*Doing well with jumping to conclusions, but I need to do more with my habit of blowing things out of proportion. Imagine scenarios of panicking in public, and think through facing the worst and putting things back into perspective.*
Facing Agoraphobia Situations	*I am ready to drive out to visit my brother.*
Facing Symptoms	*Push myself harder in exercise class; I am holding back too much.*

Figure 12.1.

Example of Completed Practice Plan

■ breathing skills;

■ thinking skills;

■ facing agoraphobia situations;

■ facing symptoms.

At the end of each week, revise your Practice Plan according to your progress and the next steps to take. This may continue for six months or more, or for as long as you want.

Long-Term Goals

You may begin long-term planning for things that you were previously unable to do because of panic and anxiety. Here are some examples of things for which you might now plan. Perhaps you have always wanted to:

■ go back to school;

■ have children;

■ meet someone new;

Practice Plan

Things to Practice	Description
Breathing Skills	
Thinking Skills	
Facing Agoraphobia Situations	
Facing Symptoms	

Long-Term Goals

Long-Term Goal	Steps to Achieve Long-Term Goal
Career move into managerial position:	*Talk to personnel staff.*
	Look at courses being offered.
	Enroll in a course.
Develop new friendships:	*Join singles groups at my church.*
	Talk to others at my gym.
	Join associations and organizations.
Going back to school:	*Call admissions office.*
	Get schedule of classes.
	Talk to others who have returned to school.

Figure 12.2.

Example of Completed Long-Term Goals Form

- travel;

- take up new hobbies;

- change jobs;

- buy a new car.

Whatever the case, consider your long-term goals and the steps needed to reach those goals. These can be revised every month.

How to Maintain Progress

There are several ways to maintain the progress that you have made so far. First, if you feel doubtful about entering certain situations or doubt that you can perform certain activities because of your fear or anxiety, that is a sign for you to go ahead and face those situations or activities.

- Use your breathing skills.

Long-Term Goals

Long-Term Goal	Steps to Achieve Long-Term Goal

■ Use your thinking strategies to help you cope with whatever it is that you are anxious about.

■ Remember, avoidance is one of the biggest causes of growing anxiety.

Second, record your mood. That is, at least once a month, consider how you have been doing in terms of your general level of anxiety and, if appropriate, your number of panic attacks. It is easier to take corrective action at an early stage rather than waiting until you are in the midst of intense panic and anxiety. Record your mood at least once a month by simply asking yourself how anxious you have felt over the last week, or how much have you been worrying about things, or whether you have had any panic attacks. It helps to tie this recording to a regular event that will remind you. Examples include monthly payment of bills or monthly meetings. Each month, record your mood just before or after such events.

Third, every now and then, review the educational information in chapters 3 and 4. Newly learned material needs to be reviewed for it to become a solid part of your way of thinking.

Your High-Risk Times

The most high-risk times for panic or anxiety to increase are stressful periods in your life. These periods can be any times in which you are under a lot of stress; whether that means job loss, the breakup of a relationship, the birth of a child, or a serious illness. Stress affects our nervous systems in ways that make us generally more tense and, therefore, causes us to have more physical symptoms and to be more likely to think negatively.

For these reasons, it is helpful to anticipate the kinds of stressful events ahead of time and to prepare for them in a matter-of-fact way.

- First, think of ways in which to manage your own anxiety. Be aware of your habits of jumping to conclusions, or blowing things out of proportion, or avoiding things.

- Second, think of concrete steps for managing the stress, such as how to deal with an angry boss or an overdue bill.

Setbacks

A panic attack or resurgence of anxiety does not mean that you are getting worse or that you have lost all of the progress that you have gained. Consider it like being on a road trip and having one of the tires on your car go flat. Yes, you need to fix the tire, but that does not mean you must go back to the beginning of your road trip. Fix the damage and continue on with your journey.

With panic and anxiety, fixing the damage means to think about what triggered the panic or anxiety, where you were jumping to conclusions or blowing things out of proportion, and how can you think more calmly and realistically. Then, continue to move forward by facing the things that made you anxious.

The most important thing to do when you have a flare-up of anxious symptoms is to repeat everything you have already done: breathing skills, thinking skills, facing agoraphobia situations, and facing symptoms.

Just because panic and anxiety have reoccurred does not mean that the treatment will not work again. It is like the old saying: if you fall off the horse, you need to dust yourself off and get back up.

For complete accounts of recent research on the nature and causes of panic and anxiety, you may wish to read David H. Barlow, *Anxiety and its disorders: The nature and treatment of anxiety and panic,* second edition (2002), and Michelle G. Craske, *Anxiety disorders: Psychological approaches to theory and treatment* (1999).

Appendix   *Answers to Self-Assessment Quizzes*

Chapter 1

1. T
2. T
3. F

4. F
5. T
6. F

Chapter 2

1. T
2. F
3. F

4. T
5. T

Chapter 3

1. T
2. F
3. F
4. F

5. T
6. F
7. F

Chapter 4

1. F
2. F
3. T

4. T
5. F
6. T

Chapter 5

1. F
2. T

3. F
4. F

Chapter 6

Section 1

1. T
2. F
3. F

4. F
5. F
6. T

Section 2

1. F
2. F

3. F
4. T

Section 3

1. F
2. F

3. T

Chapter 7

Section 2

1. F
2. T
3. F

4. T
5. F
6. T

Section 3

1. F
2. F
3. T

4. F
5. T

Section 4

1. F
2. F

3. T
4. F

Chapter 8

1. F
2. F
3. F

4. F
5. T
6. T

Chapter 9

1. F
2. T
3. T

4. F
5. F

Chapter 10

Section 1

1. T
2. F
3. T

4. F
5. F

Section 2

1. F
2. F

3. T

Section 3

1. F
2. F
3. F
4. F
5. T

Section 4

1. T
2. T
3. F
4. F

Chapter 11

1. T
2. F
3. T
4. F
5. F
6. T

References

American Psychiatric Association. (1987). *Diagnostic and statistical manual of mental disorders* (3rd ed., rev.). Washington, DC: Author.

American Psychiatric Association. (1994). *Diagnostic and statistical manual of mental disorders* (4th ed.). Washington, DC: Author.

Arntz, A., Hildebrand, M., & Van den Hout, M. (1994). Overprediction of anxiety and disconfirmatory processes in anxiety disorders. *Behaviour Research & Therapy, 32,* 709–722.

Bakker, A., van Balkom, A. J. L. M., & Spinhoven, P. (2002). SSRIs vs. TCAs in the treatment of panic disorder: A meta-analysis. *Acta Psychiatrica Scandinavica, 106,* 163–167.

Ballenger, J. C., Burrows, G. D., DuPont, R. L., Lesser, I. M., Noyes, R., Pecknold, J. C., et al. (1988). Alprazolam in panic disorder and agoraphobia: Results from a multi center trial: I. Efficacy in short-term treatment. *Archives of General Psychiatry, 45,* 413–422.

Bandura, A. (1977). Self-efficacy: Toward a unifying theory of behavioral change. *Psychological Review, 84,* 191–215.

Barlow, D. H. (2002). *Anxiety and its disorders: The nature and treatment of anxiety and panic* (2nd ed.). New York: Guilford Press.

Barlow, D. H., Brown, T. A., & Craske, M. G. (in press). Definitions of panic attacks and panic disorder in DSM–IV: Implications for research. *Journal of Abnormal Psychology.*

Barlow, D. H., Craske, M. G., Cerny, J. A., & Klosko, J. S. (1989). Behavioral treatment of panic disorder. *Behavior Therapy, 20,* 261–282.

Barlow, D. H., O'Brien, G. T., & Last, C. G. (1984). Couples' treatment of agoraphobia. *Behavior Therapy, 15,* 41–58.

Beck, A. T. (1988). Cognitive approaches to panic disorder: Theory and therapy. In S. Rachman & J. D. Maser (Eds.), *Panic: Psychological perspectives* (pp. 91–109). Hillsdale, NJ: Erlbaum.

Bouton, M. E., Mineka, S., & Barlow, D. H. (2001). A modern learning theory perspective on the etiology of panic disorder. *Psychological Review, 108,* 4–32.

Brown, T. A., Antony, M. M., & Barlow, D. H. (1995). Diagnostic comorbidity in panic disorder: Effect on treatment outcome and course of comorbid diagnoses following treatment. *Journal of Consulting & Clinical Psychology, 63,* 408–418.

Brown, T. A., & Barlow, D. H. (1995). Long-term outcome in cognitive-behavioral treatment of panic disorder: Clinical predictors and alternative strategies for assessment. *Journal of Consulting & Clinical Psychology, 63,* 754–765

Brown, T. A., DiNardo, P. A., & Barlow, D. H. (1994). *Anxiety disorders interview schedule for DSM–IV: Clinician's manual.* Albany, NY: Graywind.

Carlbring, P., Ekselius, L., & Andersson, G. (2003). Treatment of panic disorder via the Internet: A randomized trial of CBT vs. applied relaxation. *Journal of Behavior Therapy & Experimental Psychiatry, 34,* 129–140.

Carter, M. M., Turovsky, J., & Barlow, D. H. (1994). Interpersonal relationships in panic disorder with agoraphobia: A review of empirical evidence. *Clinical Psychology: Science and Practice, 164,* 759–769.

Cerny, J. A., Barlow, D. H., Craske, M. G., & Himadi, W. G. (1987). Couples' treatment of agoraphobia: A two-year follow-up. *Behavior Therapy, 18,* 401–415.

Chambless, D. L., Caputo, G. C., Bright, P., & Gallagher, R. (1984). Assessment of fear in agoraphobics: The Body Sensations Questionnaire and the Agoraphobic Cognitions Questionnaire. *Journal of Consulting & Clinical Psychology, 52,* 1090–1097.

Chambless, D. L., Sanderson, W. C., Shoham, V., Bennett Johnson, S., Pope, K. S., Crits-Christoph, P., et al. (1996). An update on empirically validated therapies. *Clinical Psychologist, 49,* 5–18.

Clark, D. M., Salkovskis, P. M., & Chalkley, A. J. (1985). Respiratory control as a treatment for panic attacks. *Journal of Behavior Therapy & Experimental Psychiatry, 16,* 23–30.

Clark, D. M., Salkovskis, P. M., Hackmann, A., Middleton, H., Anastasiades, P. & Gelder, M. (1994). Comparison of cognitive therapy, applied relaxation and imipramine in the treatment of panic disorder. *British Journal of Psychiatry, 164,* 759–769.

Clark, D. M., Salkovskis, P. M., Hackmann, A., Wells, A., Ludgate, J., & Gelder, M. (1999). Brief cognitive therapy for panic disorder: A randomized controlled trial. *Journal of Consulting & Clinical Psychology, 67,* 583–589.

Craske, M. G. (1999). *Anxiety disorders: Psychological approaches to theory and treatment.* Boulder, CO: Westview Press.

Craske, M. G. (2003). *The origins of phobias and anxiety disorders: Why more women than men.* Oxford, England: Elsevier.

Craske, M. G., Brown, T. A., & Barlow, D. H. (1991). Behavioral treatment of panic disorder: A two-year follow-up. *Behavior Therapy, 22,* 289–304.

Craske, M.G., Lang, A. J., Aikins, D., & Mystkowski, J. L. (2005). Cognitive behavioral therapy for nocturnal panic. *Behavior Therapy, 36,* 43–54.

Craske, M. G., Maidenberg, E., & Bystritsky, A. (1995). Brief cognitive-behavioral versus nondirective therapy for panic disorder. *Journal of Behavior Therapy & Experimental Psychiatry, 26,* 113–120.

Craske, M. G., Rowe, M., Lewin, M., & Noriego-Dimitri, R. (1997). Interoceptive exposure versus breathing retraining within cognitive-behavioural therapy for panic disorder with agoraphobia. *British Journal of Clinical Psychology, 36,* 85–99.

de Beurs, E., Lange, A., Van Dyck, R., & Koele, P. (1995). Respiratory training prior to exposure in vivo in the treatment of panic disorder with agoraphobia: Efficacy and predictors of outcome. *Australian & New Zealand Journal of Psychiatry, 29,* 104–113.

Deacon, B. J., & Abramowitz, J. S. (in press). A pilot study of two-day cognitive-behavioral therapy for panic disorder. *Behaviour Research & Therapy.*

Eaton, W. W., Romanoski, A., Anthony, J. C., & Nestadt, G. (1991). Screening for psychosis in the general population with a self-report interview. *Journal of Nervous & Mental Disease, 179,* 689–693.

Evans, L., Holt, C., & Oei, T. P. (1991). Long-term follow-up of agoraphobics treated by brief intensive group cognitive behavioural therapy. *Australian & New Zealand Journal of Psychiatry, 25,* 343–349.

Fava, G. A., Zielezny, M., Savron, G., & Grandi, S. (1995). Long-term effects of behavioral treatment for panic disorder with agoraphobia. *British Journal of Psychiatry, 166,* 87–92.

Foa, E. B., & Kozak, M. J. (1986). Emotional processing of fear: Exposure to corrective information. *Psychological Bulletin, 99,* 20–35.

Ghosh, A., & Marks, I. (1987). Self-treatment of agoraphobia by exposure. *Behavior Therapy, 18,* 3–16.

Gould, R. A., & Clum, G. A. (1995). Self-help plus minimal therapist contact in the treatment of panic disorder: A replication and extension. *Behavior Therapy, 26,* 533–546.

Gould, R. A., Clum, G. A., & Shapiro, D. (1993). The use of bibliotherapy in the treatment of panic: A preliminary investigation. *Behavior Therapy, 24,* 241–252.

Gould, R. A., Otto, M. W., & Pollack, M. H. (1995). A meta-analysis of treatment outcome for panic disorder. *Clinical Psychology Review, 15,* 819–844.

Katerndahl, D. A., & Realini, J. P. (1995). Where do panic attack sufferers seek care? *Journal of Family Practice, 40,* 237–243.

Katon, W., & Roy-Byrne, P. P. (1989). Panic disorder in the medically ill. *Journal of Clinical Psychiatry, 50,* 299–302.

Katon, W., Von Korff, M., Lin, E., Lipscomb, P., Russo, J., Wagner, E., et al. (1990). Distressed high utilizers of medical care: DSM-III-R diagnoses and treatment needs. *General Hospital Psychiatry, 12,* 355–362.

Keijsers, G., Schaap, C., Hooghuin, C., & Lammers, M. W. (1995). Patient-therapist interaction as a predictor of outcome in the behavioural treatment of panic disorder. *Behavior Modification, 19,* 491–517.

Kessler, R. C., Chiu, W. T., Demler, O., & Walters, E. E. (2005). Prevalence, severity, and comorbidity of 12-month DSM-IV disorders in the National Comorbidity Survey Replication. *Archives of General Psychiatry, 62,* 617–627.

Klosko, J. S., Barlow, D. H., Tassinari, R. B., & Cerny, J. A. (1990). A comparison of alprazolam and behavior therapy in treatment of panic disorder. *Journal of Consulting and Clinical Psychology, 58,* 77–84.

Leon, A. C., Portera, L., & Weissman, M. M. (1995). The social costs of anxiety disorders. *British Journal of Psychiatry, 166,* 19–22.

Lidren, D. M., Watkins, P. L., Gould, R. A., Clum, G. A., Asterino, M., & Tulloch, H. L. (1994). A comparison of bibliotherapy and group therapy in the treatment of panic disorder. *Journal of Consulting & Clinical Psychology, 62,* 865–869.

Margraf, J., Barlow, D. H., Clark, D. M., & Telch, M. J. (1993). Psychological treatment of panic: Work in progress on outcome, active ingredients, and follow-up. *Behaviour Research & Therapy, 31,* 1–8.

Marks, I. M., Swinson, R. P., Basoglu, M., Kuch, K., Noshirvani, H., O'Sullivan, G., et al. (1993). Alprazolam and exposure alone and combined in panic disorder with agoraphobia: A controlled study in London and Toronto. *British Journal of Psychiatry, 162,* 776–787.

McLean, P. D., Woody, S., Taylor, S., & Koch, W. J. (1998). Comorbid panic disorder and major depression: Implications for cognitive-behavioral therapy. *Journal of Consulting & Clinical Psychology, 66,* 240–247.

Mermelstein, H. T., & Holland, J. C. (1991). Psychotherapy by telephone: A therapeutic tool for cancer patients. *Psychosomatics: Journal of Consultation Liaison Psychiatry, 32,* 407–412.

Mitte, K. (2005). A meta-analysis of the efficacy of psycho- and pharmacotherapy in panic disorder with and without agoraphobia. *Journal of Affective Disorders, 88,* 27–45.

Morissette, S. B., Spiegel, D. A., & Heinrichs, N. (2005). Sensation-focused intensive treatment for panic disorder with moderate to severe agoraphobia. *Cognitive & Behavioral Practice, 12,* 17–29.

Neron, S., Lacroix, D., & Chaput, Y. (1995). Group vs. individual cognitive behaviour therapy in panic disorder: An open clinical trial with a six month follow-up. *Canadian Journal of Behavioural Sciences, 27,* 379–392.

Newman, M. G., Kenardy, J., Herman, S., & Taylor, C. B. (1997). Comparison of palmtop-computer-assisted brief cognitive-behavioral treatment to cognitive-behavioral treatment for panic disorder. *Journal of Consulting & Clinical Psychology, 65,* 178–183.

Ost, L. G. (1988). Applied relaxation, description of a coping technique and review of controlled studies. *Behaviour Research & Therapy, 25,* 397–410.

Otto, M. W., Jones, J. C., Craske, M. G., & Barlow, D. H. (1996). *Stopping anxiety medication: Panic control therapy for benzodiazepine discontinuation, therapist guide.* San Antonio, TX: Psychological Corporation.

Otto, M. W., Pollack, M. H., & Sabatino, S. A. (1996). Maintenance of remission following cognitive-behavior therapy for panic disorder: Possible deleterious effects of concurrent medication treatment. *Behavior Therapy, 27,* 473–482.

Otto, M. W., Pollack, M. H., Sachs, G. S., Reiter, S. R., Meltzer-Broody, S., & Rosenbaum, J. F. (1993). Discontinuation of benzodiazepine treatment: Efficacy of cognitive-behavior therapy for clients with panic disorder. *American Journal of Psychiatry, 150,* 1485–1490.

Persons, J. B. (1990). Disputing irrational thoughts can be avoidance behavior: A case report. *Behavior Therapist, 13,* 132–133.

Reiss, S., Peterson, R. A., Gursky, D. M., & McNally, R. J. (1986). Anxiety sensitivity, anxiety frequency and the prediction of fearfulness. *Behaviour Research & Therapy, 24,* 1–8.

Richards, J. C., Klein, B., & Carlbring, P. (2003). Internet-based treatment for panic disorder. *Cognitive Behaviour Therapy, 32,* 125–135.

Rijiken, H., Kraaimaat, F., De Ruiter, C., & Garssen, B. (1992). A follow-up study on short-term treatment of agoraphobia. *Behaviour Research & Therapy, 30,* 63–66.

Roy-Byrne, P. P., & Cowley, D. S. (2002). Pharmacological treatments for panic disorder, generalized anxiety disorder, specific phobia, and social anxiety disorder. In P. E. Nathan & J. M. Gorman (Eds.), *A guide to treatments that work* (2nd ed., pp. 337–365). New York: Oxford University Press.

Roy-Byrne, P. P., Craske, M. G., Stein, M. B., Sullivan, G., Bystritsky, A., Katon, W. J., et al. (2005). A randomized effectiveness trial of cognitive behavior therapy and medication for primary care panic disorder. *Archives of General Psychiatry, 62,* 290–298.[DoP1]

Roy-Byrne, P. P., Stein, M. B., Russo, J., Mercier, E., Thomas, R., McQuaid, J., et al. (1999). Panic disorder in the primary care setting. *Journal of Clinical Psychiatry, 60,* 492–499.

Schmidt, N. B., Staab, J. P., Trakowski, J. H., & Sammons, M. (1997). Efficacy of a brief psychosocial treatment for panic disorder in an active duty sample: Implications for military readiness. *Military Medicine, 162,* 123–129.

Shear, M. K., & Schulberg, H. C. (1995). Anxiety disorders in primary care. *Bulletin of the Menninger Clinic, 59*, A73–A85.

Spiegel, D. A., Brace, T. J., Gregg, S. F., & Nuzzarello, A. (1994). Does cognitive behavior therapy assist slow-taper alprazolam discontinuation in panic disorder? *American Journal of Psychiatry, 151*, 876–881.

Spitzer, R. L., Williams, J. B., Kroenke, K., Linzer, M., deGruy, F. V. III, et al. (1994). Utility of a new procedure for diagnosing mental disorders in primary care: The PRIME-MD 1000 study. *JAMA: Journal of the American Medical Association, 272*, 1749–1756.

Stein, M. B., Norton, G. R., Walker, J. R., Chartier, M. J., & Graham, R. (2000). Do selective serotonin re-uptake inhibitors enhance the efficacy of very brief cognitive behavioral therapy for panic disorder? A pilot study. *Psychiatry Research, 94*, 191–200.

Street, L., Craske, M. G., & Barlow, D. H. (1989). Sensations, cognitions, and the perception of cues associated with expected and unexpected panic attacks. *Behaviour Research & Therapy, 27*, 189–198.

Tsao, J. C., Lewin, M. R., & Craske, M. G. (1998). The effects of cognitive-behavioral therapy for panic disorder on comorbid conditions. *Journal of Anxiety Disorders, 12*, 357–371.

Tsao, J. C., Mystkowski, J., Zucker, B., & Craske, M. (2002). Effects of cognitive-behavior therapy for panic disorder on comorbid conditions: Replication and extension. *Behavior Therapy, 33*, 493–509.

Van Balkom, A. J., de Beurs, E., Koele, P., Lange, A., & Van Dyck, R. (1996). Long-term benzodiazepine use is associated with smaller treatment gain in panic disorder with agoraphobia. *Journal of Nervous & Mental Disease, 184*, 133–135.

Van den Hout, M., Arntz, A., & Hoekstra, R. (1994). Exposure-reduced agoraphobia but not panic, and cognitive therapy–reduced panic but not agoraphobia. *Behaviour Research & Therapy, 32*, 447–451.

Wardle, J., Hayward, P., Higgitt, A., Stabl, M., Blizard, R., & Gray, J. (1994). Effects of concurrent diazepam treatment on the outcome of exposure therapy in agoraphobia. *Behaviour Research & Therapy, 32*, 203–215.

Westin, D., & Morrison, K. (2001). A multidimensional meta-analysis of treatments for depression, panic, and generalized anxiety disorder: An empirical examination of the status of empirically supported therapies. *Journal of Consulting & Clinical Psychology, 69*, 875–899.

Williams, K. E., & Chambless, D. L. (1990). The relationship between therapist characteristics and outcome of in vivo exposure treatment for agoraphobia. *Behavior Therapy, 21*, 111–116.

Williams, S. L., & Falbo, J. (1996). Cognitive and performance-based treatments for panic attacks in people with varying degrees of agoraphobic disability. *Behaviour Research & Therapy, 34,* 253–264.

Wittchen, H. U., Reed, V., & Kessler, R. C. (1998). The relationship of agoraphobia and panic in a community sample of adolescents and young adults. *Archives of General Psychiatry, 55,* 1017–1024.

Wolpe, J. (1958). *Psychotherapy by reciprocal inhibition.* Stanford, CA: Stanford University Press.

Wolpe, J. (1990). *The practice of behavior therapy* (4th ed.) (Pergamon General Psychology Series, 1). Elmsford, NY: Pergamon Press.

About the Authors

David H. Barlow received his PhD from the University of Vermont in 1969 and has published over 500 articles and chapters and almost 50 books and clinical workbooks, mostly in the areas of emotional disorders and clinical research methodology. The books and workbooks have been translated into over 20 languages, including Arabic, Mandarin, and Russian.

He was formerly Professor of Psychiatry at the University of Mississippi Medical Center and Professor of Psychiatry and Psychology at Brown University and founded clinical psychology internships in both settings. He was also Distinguished Professor in the Department of Psychology at the University at Albany, State University of New York. Currently, he is Professor of Psychology, Research Professor of Psychiatry, and Director of the Center for Anxiety and Related Disorders at Boston University.

Barlow is the recipient of the 2000 American Psychological Association (APA) Distinguished Scientific Award for the Applications of Psychology. He is also the recipient of the First Annual Science Dissemination Award from the Society for a Science of Clinical Psychology of the APA and recipient of the 2000 Distinguished Scientific Contribution Award from the Society of Clinical Psychology of the APA. He also received an award in appreciation of outstanding achievements from the General Hospital of the Chinese People's Liberation Army, Beijing, China, with an appointment as Honorary Visiting Professor of Clinical Psychology. During the 1997–1998 academic year, he was Fritz Redlich Fellow at the Center for Advanced Study in Behavioral Sciences in Palo Alto, California.

Other awards include Career Contribution Awards from the Massachusetts, California, and Connecticut Psychological Associations; the 2004 C. Charles Burlingame Award from the Institute of Living in Hartford, Connecticut; the First Graduate Alumni Scholar Award from the Graduate College of the University of Vermont; the Masters and Johnson Award from the Society for Sex Therapy and Research; the G. Stanley Hall Lectureship, American Psychological Association; a certificate of appreciation for contributions to women in clinical psychology from Section IV of Division 12 of the APA, the Clinical Psychology of Women; and a MERIT award from the National Institute of Mental Health (NIMH) for long-term contributions to clinical research efforts. He is Past President of the Society of Clinical Psychology of the APA and the Association for the Advancement of Behavior Therapy, Past Editor of the journals *Behavior Therapy, Journal of Applied Behavior Analysis,* and *Clinical Psychology: Science & Practice,* and currently Editor-in-Chief of the Treatments*That-Work*™ series for Oxford University Press.

He was Chair of the APA Task Force of Psychological Intervention Guidelines, was a member of the DSM-IV Task Force of the APA, and was a co-chair of the work group for revising the anxiety disorder categories. He is also a Diplomate in Clinical Psychology of the American Board of Professional Psychology and maintains a private practice.

Michelle G. Craske received her PhD from the University of British Columbia in 1985 and has published more than 200 articles and chapters in the area of anxiety disorders. She has written books on the topics of the etiology and treatment of anxiety disorders, gender differences in anxiety, and translation from the basic science of fear learning to the clinical application of understanding and treating phobias, in addition to several self-help books. In addition, she has been the recipient of continuous NIMH funding since 1991 for research projects pertaining to risk factors for anxiety disorders and depression among children and adolescents, the cognitive and physiological aspects of anxiety and panic attacks, and the development and dissemination of treatments for anxiety and related disorders. She is Associate Editor for the *Journal of Abnormal Psychology* and *Behaviour Research & Therapy,* and she is a Scientific Board Member for the Anxiety Disorders Association of America. She was a member of the DSM-IV Anxiety Disorders Work Group Subcommittee for revision of the diagnostic criteria surrounding panic disorder and specific phobia. Craske has given invited keynote addresses at many international conferences and frequently is invited to present training workshops on the most recent advances in the cognitive behavioral treatment for anxiety disorders. She is currently a Professor in the Department of Psychology and Department of Psychiatry and Biobehavioral Sciences at the University of California, Los Angeles, and Director of the UCLA Anxiety Disorders Behavioral Research Program.